WAR FROM THE REAR

"Ukraine's remarkable resistance to Russia's invasion is a true people's war. This is a country that does not look to politicians to tell them what to do. The country survives because people take agency and work with each other to get weapons to the front, supply hospitals, organise partisan movements and help refugees. Lyubka tells the stories of soccer players and coffee roasters, priests and Roma who are all playing their role in this great community of resistance. In the thing once known as 'the West,' we often lament the loss of community—in Ukraine, it is thriving and winning against the invasion of a cruel Empire. Lyubka brings it alive in prose that is unsentimental yet totally inspiring."

—Peter Pomerantsev, author of *This is Not Propaganda*

"An author and a war. A real-life autobiographical road movie by and about a writer who supplied the army with 400 jeeps. An amazing story about amazing people. How do you deliver 400 jeeps to the front lines for the Ukrainian army and stay alive? In this book, you will find answers to questions you don't yet know exist. This book is an eye-opener about the extraordinary interaction between the front and the rear in Ukraine, from iconic writer Andriy Lyubka, who became one of the initiators of army crowdfunding."

—Andrey Kurkov, author of *Death and the Penguin*

WAR FROM THE REAR

A Ukrainian Aid Volunteer's Story

Andriy Lyubka

Translated from the Ukrainian
by Yulia Lyubka and Kate Tsurkan

2025

Funded by
the European Union

The translation and publication of this book are supported by the European Union under the House of Europe programme.

Copyright © Academic Studies Press, 2025, English Translation

Print LCCN 2025030434

ISBN 9798887198408 (paperback)
ISBN 9798887198415 (Adobe PDF)
ISBN 9798887198422 (ePub)

Book design by Lapiz Digital Services
Cover design by Mari Kinovych
Photographs by Andriy Lyubka

Published by Cherry Orchard Books, and imprint of Academic Studies Press
Academic Studies Press - Europe
V. Reimani tn. 5a
Tallinn, Kesklinna linnaosa, 10124, Estonia
press@academicstudiespress.com
www.academicstudiespress.com

To my beloved wife Yulia, who selflessly took over family matters while I plunged into volunteering.

Contents

Roasted Uganda	1
Cars	8
Sausage	12
Roma	15
Sleeping in the Vienna Airport toilet	20
Techyk	26
Hose	29
Khrestyshche	33
Baptists	38
Air raid in Bakhmut	45
On the road	49
The story I will never write	52
Hazelnut	57
Humor that heals us	60
The smirk of the beast	67
A moment of truth	71
The stranger	73
Evacuation	79
Kill lists	85
Over Achilles's grave	90
Orientalism	95
Bizarre deviations	100
Investments	107
Flowers of victory	108
Odesa	111
A wartime queen	113

The main thing is to survive until September	118
The cultural front	121
Degradation	124
War is not only about heroes	129
Draft	141
A country of young widows	154
Astamur Humba ("Abkhaz")	157
Youth	162
Batia	165
An icon painter	168
Postscriptum	172
Acknowledgements	173

Preface

War on the other side of the ocean
Foreword to the American edition of the book "War from the Rear"

I flew from New York back home to Ukraine exactly one week before the US presidential election. My friends assured me that the situation was still uncertain and there was still a chance, but in reality, it was already clear that Trump would win and the world was entering a new era.

My tour of Canada and the US was dedicated to the role of culture during the war in Ukraine. I talked about my volunteer work, but generally focused on the enormous role that culture plays in shaping identity and strengthening the spirit of unity in a society going through a tragic period in its history.

In North America, many people found my ideas, if not maximalist, then at least romantic. I emphasized that the deep roots of Ukrainian resistance lie primarily in culture. Not only in high culture such as literature or music, but above all in everyday culture, which forms horizontal connections between people, creates trust between them, and builds community. After all, culture is the foundation of the values we are fighting for.

A writer who can raise a million dollars to help the army in a poor country during a war is not about literature, but about trust. It is about the fact that in difficult times, culture is more resilient than politics because it unites regardless of any divisions.

Joint resistance is not about politics, but about values, among which freedom is a priority. In this light, culture emerges as a strategic element of the security system, because it unites the community and creates an invisible demarcation line that distinguishes and separates us from the invaders. We do not want to be with them or under their rule, because freedom, democracy, and our own identity are important to us. In Ukraine, in the third year of full-scale invasion, this was obvious and banal, but in America it sounded like a romantic fairy tale.

All the political and geopolitical consequences we have seen from November 2024 to the present day are only the tip of the iceberg. Its larger and more important underwater part lies in the neglect and abandonment of culture, in its commercialization and marginalization. If culture becomes only entertainment for society or a "game of beads" for a small elite, political changes are inevitable. After all, we see this ourselves every day.

There is a bitter joke in Ukraine based on the difference in time zones: Ukrainians should go to sleep before Trump wakes up on the other side of the ocean and starts making his statements. Because if you don't go to sleep, you'll read about it and definitely won't be able to sleep.

The full-scale Russian invasion and the phenomenal resistance of Ukrainians have significantly changed the discourse in which Ukraine and "Ukrainian issues" exist. If, during thirty years of independence, everyone around us taught us how to live and how to reform, then after 2022 it suddenly turned out that we can also teach the world something. To share our experience and secrets of resilience.

The book you are now holding in your hands is not about war or cars for the front. It is merely a backdrop against which I tell everyday human stories, share examples from life in extreme situations, and show how strong and existentially necessary the vitalistic role of culture is. Culture that is about values, respect for others, and trust.

In Ukrainian, when we talk about something commonplace and banal, we say, "I'm not going to reveal America to you." So in this book, I'm not going to "reveal America to you," but I will show how the American example of the ideal of freedom and democracy captivated us, taught us, prepared us, and shaped us.

This ideal is so powerful for us that we can now share it with America itself. Because culture is a two-way street; it is about exchange, mutual support, and dialogue. And no ocean can interrupt this dialogue.

Roasted Uganda

Of all the things I took to the front for Ukrainian soldiers, the most important was a pack of coffee—a one-kilogram roll of freshly roasted beans from a hipster coffeehouse-roastery in downtown Uzhhorod. The rectangular, shiny package with a trendy "Roasted Uganda" sticker looked more suited for Instagram than the front lines.

It served a purely defensive function, though it helped protect not the body, but something more important than the body—what makes us human. When I used to write poetry, I would have called this strange substance the soul, but now I'll use a more prosaic, yet more accurate term. That coffee helped protect the psyche, creating the sense that you were not just a piece of meat, a target for snipers and bombs, but a person—a person with tastes, preferences, and habits.

I clearly remember that morning—early May, when the nights are still cold, but the air quickly warms with the morning and its scents. A village somewhere beyond Sloviansk in Donbas, where there are now far fewer locals than soldiers. Most people have left because the outskirts are shelled almost daily, and at night, it's impossible to sleep because of the explosions. Explosions are easier to hear at night, by the way—they take on a certain depth, sounding ominously in the dark silence, like a foreign heartbeat.

That time, our volunteer team arrived at the military unit's location too late. We were delayed at the checkpoints, the road was tough, and because we had a poor mobile signal, we got a bit lost on unfamiliar routes. We arrived when it wasn't fully dark yet, but it was already that point in the evening when you'd want to turn on some lights. This meant we would have to spend the night with the soldiers, as leaving at night was impossible because of the light camouflage protocol. The online maps were down, the area was unfamiliar to us, and it was forbidden to use headlights—so in this situation, we could easily have ended up driving onto Russian positions.

And after a brief and restless sleep, interrupted by the sounds of explosions both near and far, we woke up, ready to quickly head off to the next unit. However, my friend, who had put on a military uniform after February 24, stopped us. "Wait," he said. "I'll make some coffee."

There was no electricity, so he started up a diesel generator, connected a small coffee machine, poured in water, and then, from the box I had delivered to him the day before, took out a pack of coffee. "Roasted Uganda," the label read. He scooped it into the coffee machine—and within a minute, the cool May morning air was filled with the aroma of premium Arabica.

I think that's probably how the Bible was written. When Jesus started distributing fish and bread to the crowd, they couldn't have been more astonished than we were at that moment. It was a genuine miracle: in one of the world's most dire places, somewhere near Sloviansk in Donbas, in the middle of a war, holding a metal mug with perfectly brewed espresso. It was probably the most delicious coffee of my life. It might sound clichéd, but it's true.

With a knowing grin, my friend made a theatrical pause before responding to the unspoken question on our minds:

"Maybe I'll die today. Why should it be a day when I didn't have my usual morning coffee? Fuck them—I'm not giving up my coffee. No damn Putin is going to take that away from me. I'm used to starting my morning with good espresso, so at least that's one thing I'm entitled to, isn't it?"

Since then, I've traveled to different military units about fifteen more times—to the north, near the Russian border in Kharkiv oblast; to the south, near Kherson, in the liberated areas of Ukraine's Black Sea region. As for Donbas, I probably know it better now than my native Transcarpathia.

In short, I've seen and heard a lot in these months, but that phrase has stayed with me. Because it's about something more fundamental than geopolitics, theaters of war, or newsfeeds. It's about the essential human right to preserve one's individuality, one's sense of self, one's unique identity among hundreds of thousands of others. The right not to dissolve into the anonymous mass of the millions of Ukrainian soldiers defending their homeland but to remain a singular being—one of a kind.

Imagine a person who, before February 24, was just a civilian, perhaps even a latent pacifist, and after the full-scale invasion found themselves on the front lines. Their entire life has been upended—they've been torn away from family and home, their job and social circle, their routines and the ability to plan for the future. Dressed in camouflage that not only blends them into a million other soldiers but also with the surrounding landscape, this person—no matter how thick their body armor—is suddenly stripped bare to the bone. They have nothing left that defines them as an individual; their flesh and blood are entirely devoted to the shared, collective goal.

And so, another battle begins—a battle for the right to be oneself, to have one's own preferences, and to cling to a cherished routine at an extraordinary cost. Drinking your favorite coffee in the morning feels like coming home—it's comforting, like spending cherished time with family. It's a moment to simply be yourself. It's just three minutes a day—not for grand purposes, not for the state, not as a statistic—but solely for you.

Yes, this is yet another war—a silent war for personal time. Dozens of soldiers have told me that during combat shifts in trenches and bunkers, they actively read. They catch up on books they missed in university and dive into modern bestsellers about marketing and the history of business empires. They read because it gives them a sense that these days are not wasted, that they are using them for personal growth.

War takes everything from us, but most of all, it robs us of our time—those productive years often called "the prime of life." This time is lost forever. So what else can civilians who find themselves in the trenches by a twist of fate do, if not try to seize this time, to snatch a small piece of it for their own lives? That's why soldiers on the front lines use smartphone apps to learn German, read about the history of the IKEA corporation, or take driving lessons right next to the battlefield. It's an attempt to ensure that the time of war isn't entirely wasted.

Yes, I know it's self-deception, but it helps people hold on. Perhaps this understanding is the reason I visit our soldiers on the front lines. It all started in April, when my friend—a civilian just yesterday but now a soldier—called me. During our conversation, he casually mentioned that what their unit needed most was a four-wheel drive vehicle.

Since the war began, the Ukrainian army has grown sevenfold. While soldiers were recruited and equipped with uniforms and rifles, the newly formed units remain poorly supplied with vehicles. They might rely on massive trucks or outdated buses, with no mobile, off-road transport available.

Take, for example, a unit from my hometown, Uzhhorod. In early March, this newly formed battalion was sent to Donbas. As a newly formed unit, essentially existing only "on paper," it had no transport whatsoever. To get them moving, they were given an old school bus. Uzhhorod is closer to Venice than to Donbas, so it's no surprise that the rickety yellow bus broke down along the way. The soldiers spent nearly a day in the freezing cold waiting for a replacement. But in the chaotic first days of March, no help was sent.

In the end, these soldiers—who, just two weeks earlier, were civilians—pooled their own money and traveled the last two hundred kilometers to Donbas by taxi. A Ukrainian soldier heading to the front by taxi—this, too, is a symbol of the war.

When I heard from my friend at the beginning of spring 2022 that their unit desperately needed a jeep, I felt a natural urge to help. I thought about reaching out to acquaintances or charity organizations that could quickly address the issue, but soon realized that no one would act quickly enough. In other words, I had to stop searching for charitable organizations and start looking in the mirror—I had to take matters into my own hands. That same evening, I posted on Facebook that I was collecting funds to buy a jeep for a military unit in Donbas and shared my bank card details. When I woke up, my account had enough money for two jeeps.

And that's how my current responsibility in this war came to be. Since April 2022, I've stopped being a writer, as I hardly write anything these days. Instead, I raise funds and buy jeeps for the Ukrainian army. My team and I repair them, paint them in camouflage colors, and deliver them straight to the front lines. As of today, I have purchased 211 vehicles for the Armed Forces of Ukraine. More to come.

Thanks to my readers, this has all been possible—those who once read my books and attended my book events, and who now support my volunteer work with their donations. For a writer, there's a special kind of satisfaction and validation in seeing your readers trust you in real life, understanding that the books you wrote have helped build a strong, if unseen, community. A writer who no longer writes—this, too, might be a symbol of the war. I sometimes joke that my readers donate with such zeal because they want me to focus on cars and never write again.

Although I do have something to write about. When we travel east with a convoy of jeeps, which takes a day and a half one way, I have plenty of time for thoughts and daydreams. During those hours, I imagine my first postwar book. It will be about everything in the world—except cars. After the war, I'll buy a bicycle and won't even look at cars anymore, I'll be so done with them. And I'll write a lot, making up for the pause forced by the war.

I will write about people, human experiences, and the situations and voices that shape them. I'll write about war as a personal experience, not just a geopolitical catastrophe. I'll share the fear I felt traveling for the first time from peaceful Uzhhorod to the front lines of Donbas. But when I arrived, I realized that in the proximity of war, fear disappears, because fear is more of an internal feeling than a matter of geography.

I will write about one of the drivers on our team, who, during a stop in Sloviansk, was preparing sandwiches for us and cut his hand while opening a tin can. Fifty years from now, when his grandchildren ask him, "Grandpa, what did you do during the war?" he will be able to answer truthfully, "I can't say much, but I'll tell you this: I spilled my blood in Sloviansk."

I won't write about the conversation when a soldier, who had come home on a short leave, had too much to drink and confided in me: "You know, there's only one thing I want. This is an artillery war, most of the time we sit in the trenches and pray we don't get bombed. I've been at war for nine months, and I still haven't had a Russian in my sights. So, I'm afraid a bomb will fall on me—and I'll die. I'm ready to die, I'm not afraid of death. I'm afraid of dying from a bomb, in my sleep, at lunch, at the table, or—God forbid—

on the toilet. A bomb doesn't choose where it falls. I went to war and accepted the possibility of death, but I ask for just one thing: let me die by human hands, not from a bomb. Let me see the enemy with my own eyes. May God grant me this final human mercy—to die by the hands of a person. Is that too much to ask?"

Cars

———

I never would have believed that someday I'd be working with cars—it's like a joke that doesn't get any funnier no matter how many times you repeat it. If someone had told me two years ago that my main area of interest would be large four-wheel drive vehicles, I would have thought they were nuts.

The world has truly gone mad, so instead of writing novels, this writer started raising money, searching for SUVs all over the world, and buying them by the hundred for the needs of the Ukrainian army. It's important to note that all of this happened by chance, almost like it happened on its own.

The paradox is that I am indifferent to cars. Before the war, I had two personal vehicles: a compact city car and an SUV, which I used for fishing trips or family vacations. I had ten years of driving experience and nearly two hundred thousand kilometers under my belt. But cars interested me only as a means of comfortable travel and flexible route planning, not as technical mechanisms.

I mean, I enjoy driving, the romance of the road, and the ease of traveling that a car offers. But I couldn't care less what's under the hood: what kind of engine it has, what potential issues it might have, how much horsepower it has, or whether it's a body-on-frame construction. In my opinion, the mechanic should be the one looking under the hood, and overall, the best car is the one whose hood you never need to look under in the first place.

Fate arranged it so that I learned the difference between the construction of diesel and gasoline engines, became skilled at checking the performance of injectors, and assessing the condition of all-wheel drive systems. Moreover, after buying over two hundred cars for the armed forces, I now know the typical structural flaws of certain models. Mercedes cars tend to rust over time, Mitsubishi L200s have radiator issues, and Nissan Navaras weaken at the driveshaft. I know that a 1.9-liter engine is too small for the front line—better to go for a 2.4 or even a 2.5. I learned that, for field conditions, a manual transmission is more functional, durable, and cheaper to repair than an automatic. I figured out that belts can squeal "when cold," and after a few minutes, that sound disappears. I can tell potential car malfunctions by the color of smoke from the exhaust pipe. I reluctantly became the holder of all this knowledge, though I would have preferred to study the evolution of uniform temperament in Baroque symphonic music.

The fact that cars are far from my passion doesn't mean that this volunteer work doesn't bring me satisfaction. On the contrary, by getting involved in supplying vehicles to the units at the front lines, I found fulfillment because I felt useful.

In the first days and weeks of the war, I received dozens of invitations for publications and interviews with global media. Every editorial wanted an author's piece on the experience of the war, an explanation of its causes, an essay by a Ukrainian writer who was, so to speak, in the thick of events. But it was exactly at that moment that I'd reached an impasse and couldn't write anything. The anxiety swirling in my mind made it impossible to focus and follow any logical train of thought.

But there was also a much more significant reason: I had lost faith in words. For me, the start of the full-scale invasion felt like a personal defeat, a private failure as a writer and columnist. As a representative of the cohort of people who write and formulate meanings. When the first missiles fell on peaceful, sleeping cities, it became clear that words were powerless and empty—the time for weapons had come. In the first months of the war, I didn't just feel apathy, I felt a real disgust for writing: it seemed selfish and meaningless to me.

It was a time when I wanted to make a tangible difference, not just offer words or chatter about "important messages in foreign media." So I focused on what I could do: first, I helped house refugees from Ukrainian cities that had been shelled or had fallen under occupation.

Then I found an even more rewarding job—I worked as a loader. Hundreds of trucks with humanitarian aid for Ukraine were arriving in my border region of Transcarpathia, so I helped unload them and send the supplies further east. Later, we set up something like a bridge between western Ukraine's Uzhhorod and eastern Ukraine's Kharkiv: I received the most essential goods from the Medical Aid Committee, loaded the boxes and bags onto trains, and sent them to my fellow author Serhiy Zhadan's team in Kharkiv. It may sound paradoxical, but the physical labor gave me a sense of relief. With my own hands, I could touch the aid—it had weight and real shape, and someone was eating it, healing with it, covering themselves, or warming up with it. Moreover, the exhaustion from physical work brought a deep, peaceful sleep, the kind of sleep you get when you know you've earned your day. And busy hands meant I didn't have time to check my phone every minute for distressing news. In short, there were many benefits.

Then came the cars, and everything spun around, shifting my life onto a new track. And I felt even more relief, because these cars were big and powerful, and they were desperately needed at the front. Not only could you touch them, you could drive them! These vehicles evacuated the wounded from under shelling, delivered ammunition to positions, and assisted in the offensive. In my view, during these critical months of the war, this kind of help was far more valuable than a patriotic poem or anthem that might lift spirits, or an article about the war's truth that a few hundred thousand Danes might read in their daily newspaper, or a speech about the horrors of Russian crimes at some German forum, followed by an audience relaxing with a glass of wine.

In these terrifying times, writing and creativity took a backseat for me. The most important thing became the cars and helping the army. As a writer, philologist, and passionate reader, I believe this was absolutely the right priority.

Sausage

Truth be told, my volunteer work was originally supposed to be limited to sending sausages. Somehow, though, I took an unexpected turn and found myself working with cars. Although it all began with sausages.

It was April 2022. I got together with my friends Andriy and Dmytro to discuss the latest developments of the war and how we could help the army in the best way possible. We recalled a friend of ours, a civilian who had joined the ranks of the Transcarpathian Territorial Defense Forces and was already entrenched in Donbas with his unit for the past month.

Easter was approaching, and even staunch atheists like me found themselves preparing for the holiday. After all, I'm an atheist, not a fool, and those holidays on the church calendar tied to culinary feasts are ones I celebrate with enthusiasm. In Transcarpathia, Easter is the culinary highlight, the pinnacle of everything that can be best served on the table.

In the Transcarpathian Easter basket, alongside the Easter bread (*paska*) and painted eggs (*pysanky*), there are always two other delicacies: smoked sausage and *shovdar*. The latter is a massive pig's leg that's cured in salt and then smoked. It's served boiled and sliced into thick pieces. It's our Transcarpathian version of prosciutto and *jamón*, only, of course, better.

The second delicacy in the basket, the sausage, is a true masterpiece. In Transcarpathia, everyone has their "own" butcher, just like others have their "own" hairdresser, doctor, or manicurist. This sausage is made by hand, and while its recipe is both closely guarded and widely known, knowing the recipe isn't enough—you have to have the right touch.

It's important that the sausage is properly smoked. You can only do this with branches and wood dust from fruit trees, and not just any fruit trees, but only those that bear stone fruits, like apricots or cherries. The smoke from these trees is highly aromatic and gives the sausage a certain lightness. I always said that sausage is the best dessert, and when smoked this way, it turns into a weapon of mass seduction. Anyone who enters the zone of its fragrance automatically becomes religious and eagerly awaits the celebration of Christ's Resurrection.

My friends and I decided that *shovdar* and sausage absolutely had to be on the table of a Transcarpathian soldier, so that there, on the front lines in Donbas, he could taste the flavor of home and know he was not forgotten back on the homestead front. We decided to pool our money to buy fifty kilograms of *shovdar* and as much sausage, enough not only for our friend but for his entire unit. A few minutes later, I had everything arranged with the butcher, and in my excitement, I called my soldier friend in Donbas.

His reply slightly deflated my high spirits: "Thanks, but how are we going to get this sausage to Donbas? There are no DHL couriers to the front, no Nova Poshta offices in the trenches, and the nearest inhabited settlement is dozens of kilometers away. There's no way to get there because my unit is infantry and has no mobile transport. If only we had a jeep..."

Within an hour, I posted a call on Facebook to raise funds for a jeep for the troops in Donbas, and by morning, I had enough for two. And that's how my journey with purchasing vehicles began.

Ah, I could have been a sausage volunteer! How much better my life could have been: instead of buying old, battered cars, I could have been buying delicious and fragrant sausages. I can imagine my reports a year into my volunteer work: "Friends, thank you for your donations! Yesterday, we acquired our 153rd ton of sausage and sent it to the southern front! We also purchased two pallets of liver pâté and twenty boxes of smoked bacon with meat streaks! Glory to Ukraine! We're working for victory!"

Imagine the great photos: a platoon of soldiers, thirty sun-kissed men with strong faces and full gear—and each one with a slice of sausage on the barrel of their rifle! Or picture this: paratroopers sitting at a table, each with an empty plate in front of them. Their faces are content, happy—no pretense, no coercion.

People from villages send me goats, chickens, and cows to support our volunteer efforts. I would set up a large ranch outside Uzhhorod, where I would raise cattle and other livestock, preparing for winter and the tough times ahead at the front. Makers of Cossack mustard would become our official sponsors, and bakers would line up to supply every batch of our products with fresh bread.

Meanwhile, our volunteer team would work tirelessly, hands and forks always in motion. Every batch of sausages, canned goods, and bacon would be carefully checked to ensure it's safe for the soldiers. As they say, we work without sparing ourselves—and with each passing month, the smiles in our photos would get bigger and brighter. Now that's what I call volunteering, not some rusty old clunkers!

Roma

Few people probably realize that, after the United States, Slovak Roma are the second largest contributors to the aid delivered to the Ukrainian army.

I'm confident that Roma from Hungary, Romania, and even Germany are supporting us, and Ukrainian Roma are courageously fighting for their country. However, it's the Slovak Roma who are most effectively involved in the supply chain for the Ukrainian army. Not all of them, of course, but at least three. In fact, most of the cars I purchased with public funds were delivered to us from England by them. So, this story will focus on the main one among them—Mr. František.

In early June 2022, when my volunteer work was gaining momentum, I was sitting and browsing websites of neighboring countries looking for old jeeps and pickups that could be bought for the Ukrainian army. And I came across a strange ad for a cheap pickup truck in the Slovak city of Michalovce, which is just forty kilometers from Uzhhorod. It was a 2008 Ford Ranger. Such a vehicle should have cost around six to eight thousand euros, but the price listed on the website was just over four thousand. There had to be some catch, but the car was so close to me that I decided to go check it out myself.

After arranging a time to inspect the vehicle over the phone, I set off for Slovakia. In Michalovce, in the parking lot near a large supermarket, I was greeted by three Roma. The pickup wasn't there, and they told me I needed to drive with them to a place nearby where the car was. "Here's the catch," I thought to myself, and my imagination immediately painted

a picture of stolen money and my dismembered body at the bottom of the local Shiravske reservoir. I had nearly bought into all the stereotypes.

But since I had been waiting in line at the border for over four hours, I decided to follow the Roma, who, for added drama, arrived in a BMW with tinted windows. The absurdity of the situation was heightened by the fact that the fancy BMW had the steering wheel on the right side—an old joke about a bus running the Khust-Tokyo route suddenly came to mind.

Ten minutes later, we arrived at an elegant-looking house with a spacious yard, where the Ford Ranger really did shine in the sun. I approached and inspected it. At first glance, it seemed like an ordinary car, but with one detail: the steering wheel was also on the right side. "Did you import it from Japan through Odesa?" I asked, remembering that in the past, right-hand drive cars would make their way to Ukraine this way. "No, it's an English car" is how they explained the obvious.

I took the key and went for a drive: the car ran smoothly, the engine hummed evenly, the interior was reasonably well maintained, and overall, for its age, it looked good. The right-hand drive, though, was a bit of an oddity. But, in the end, it wasn't such a big issue, especially in wartime. The main thing was that it worked—on the front lines, there are no traffic cops or stoplights.

We started talking, and the Roma explained everything to me. It turned out the English car had made its way to this part of the world by chance—they had driven it here from England. When Slovakia joined the European Union in 2004, people from the poorer eastern part of the country flooded into other member states to work. Among them were the Eastern Slovak Roma. Many of them settled in Germany, but the most determined ones made their way to Foggy Albion, where they found employment and started a new life.

One of these people was Mr. František, the father of a large Roma family. He has been living between two countries for almost twenty years—working in England, where he has all the paperwork and even medical insurance. His children attended school there and speak English fluently. But he is always drawn back home, so he invested his earnings from the UK into building a truly grand house in his native Michalovce. In England, he could have bought a small apartment, but in Eastern Slovakia, he built a nice villa.

The thing is, low-cost airlines sell tickets from Eastern Europe to London for just ten euros, but the prices in the opposite direction can be astronomical, especially with luggage. English people often put almost new electronics and quality items out on the sidewalk, which catch the eyes and hands of Eastern Europeans. To bring this treasure home, you need a large vehicle. That's why Roma buy cheap old pickups, load them up like camels, and drive across the whole continent. This is how the mentioned Ford Ranger ended up in the eastern Slovak town.

Right-hand-drive cars are very difficult or expensive to register in countries with left-hand traffic, which is why such cars cost at least a third less than regular ones. And it was this tempting price that led me to one of these cars on a Roma yard in Michalovce in June 2022.

Since then, using the "Roma channel," which, like the English Channel, connects England and Uzhhorod, I've bought over a hundred cars for the Ukrainian army from František. Besides the price, they have another important advantage: the Roma drive them from England, meaning the car passes a durability test over a 2,500-kilometer stretch. If it makes it to Uzhhorod, it will make it to Donbas, and then to the victory parade through the Moscow swamps.

There would be nothing particularly special about this story if it weren't for the fact that the cars are brought to me by Slovak Roma. When Hungarians, Romanians, Poles, or Lithuanians bring cars, that's fine, but the mention of Roma evokes a full spectrum of emotions in everyone, from laughter to disdain. I admit, during that first meeting by the tinted BMW, I almost became a victim of stereotypes myself.

And it's a good thing I didn't, because it later turned out that Roma can be trusted and worked with. For example, there were several times when a car brought by "our people" arrived without a stereo, spare tire, or jack—and in my experience, there was never a situation where the Roma took anything from the car for themselves.

So, I hope that at the victory parade, which will take place somewhere in the area of what used to be Moscow, between Zelensky and Biden, there will be a seat for Mr. František—an honest Slovak Roma.

Sleeping in the Vienna Airport toilet

―――――

Once, I was asked to describe a typical day as a volunteer. At the time, I rambled something vague, trying to evoke sympathy by highlighting the overwhelming workload, but now I've remembered one particular day that vividly captures the pendulum-like nature of my life and volunteer work. Let me tell you about a specific day, from October 4th to 5th, 2022.

For context, the day before, I had been with my team in Donbas and the recently liberated part of Kharkiv region, delivering seven jeeps and one minibus for Ukrainian military units. A trip from Uzhhorod and back takes almost four full days: we usually leave on Friday evening and return on Monday. During this time, we only have one full night of sleep; the rest of the time, we nap in the cars, taking turns at the wheel. Naturally, after such a trip—3,500 kilometers and four days on the road, not to mention the stress of being in a frontline zone—a person returns home in a kind of somnambulistic state. "As if taken down from the Cross" is how we put it in my family.

After returning from another volunteer trip to the east on Monday evening, I still had to take the bus to the car wash, sort and throw the clothes in for washing, and pack for the next day . . . I went to bed late and woke up very early because I had little time and a lot of work: I needed to visit all the service stations, inspect the car repairs, pay for the work, and coordinate spare parts orders (one for each of the four jeeps, separately, from different suppliers).

Later, I needed to take care of financial matters, including gathering the money I'd received from people and exchanging it for euros, as that evening I had to inspect and buy three more cars abroad for the Ukrainian military. Caught up in the traffic jams of a city overflowing with internally displaced people, I didn't have time for lunch, so I just grabbed a hot dog at the gas station. Immediately after, I rushed to the Uzhhorod bus station, where children and a TV crew were waiting for me.

The children were students at a music school, and their teacher, Ms. Maria, would gather them each week and take them to perform in public places, such as squares or supermarket halls, where they sang songs to raise money for the army. Part of these funds were transferred to my account, and to encourage and entertain the children, we invited them to the transport company and let them paint the military bus in camouflage colors. This bus had been purchased with the money they raised, so the symbolism of the event was extraordinary. It's no surprise that a team from a TV channel wanted to travel from the capital to film the occasion.

I had to manage what felt like a traveling circus: the quiet, gruff car mechanics, my fellow volunteers, the music school teachers, children ranging from five to fifteen, their parents anxiously watching over them, and journalists with cameras and microphones. Juggling it all—one group singing patriotic songs, another crying because their paintbrushes were taken, a third running from the cameras in embarrassment, and a fourth chasing everyone around with their own cameras—was quite the experience.

But I pulled it off, and two hours later, without going home, I headed to a village near Uzhhorod where there's a pedestrian border crossing to Slovakia. I crossed the border in about an hour, and on the other side, I was met by the Slovak Roma, Mr. František, about whom you read a few pages earlier. By the time we reached the town of Michalovce, it was already dark.

In Michalovce, I spent nearly two hours checking the cars brought by František: I drove each one into the field outside the city, tested the all-wheel drive, engine, and fuel system, checked the suspension and the integrity of the frame. Then I settled up with František and called members of my team, arranging who and when would bring these cars to Uzhhorod.

I was desperately tired and about to fall asleep, but František insisted that I visit him for a moment. He said his family rarely gathers in Michalovce, but now they were all there, and it would be a great honor for them if I came, even for just tea. As I understood later, František simply wanted to show off his house: it truly impressed with its wealth and colorful style.

After drinking tea and expressing my admiration for the host's house, I asked to be taken to Košice. The drive there took an hour, and we arrived just before midnight. In Košice, I had a brief meeting with someone who wanted to sell an ambulance. By the time we finished, it was already after two in the morning, and my flight was at four. So, I just bought a beer and sat on a bench in the city center to catch my breath. Then I called a taxi and headed to the airport.

I was flying to Tirana, Albania, for the opening of the largest literary festival in the country, the Tirana Gate International Literary Festival. To be honest, any other person would have refused such an invitation, because representing Ukraine should be done in Berlin or New York, in world capitals, but I find that approach to be a reflection of provincial inferiority, which is worth discussing another time in the context of decolonization. We demand respect and attention from the world, but smaller countries receive the same haughty indifference that larger ones give us. As a Balkanist by training, I felt a sort of professional duty to fly to Tirana and ensure the

Ukrainian voice was heard there. After all, Albania, perhaps more than any other country in the Balkans, supports Ukraine passionately, so it was only fitting to go and express gratitude in person.

I flew from Košice, the closest airport to Uzhhorod, to Tirana with a layover in Vienna. The flight from Košice to Vienna is just forty minutes, so you barely have time to sit down and fasten your seatbelt before the plane begins its descent. Needless to say, I didn't manage to sleep on the plane. In Vienna, there was a gray, rainy October dawn, and I was in the middle of yet another sleepless night. There were four and a half hours left before my flight to Tirana, and I could no longer keep myself on my feet.

So, I did something I'm ashamed of, but don't regret. I can't sleep in public; I feel that a person is too vulnerable when they're asleep, and I don't want random strangers to see me like that. So, at Vienna Airport, I found a restroom for people with disabilities, went inside, and locked the door. I set an alarm on my phone, lowered the toilet seat, sat on it, placed my small suitcase on my lap, laid my jacket over it, and rested my head on top. I fell asleep instantly and slept like a baby for three hours. I woke up, washed my face, and walked like a zombie to check in for my flight.

On the plane, I had two coffees, but they only sped up my heartbeat. Then I drank two small bottles of white wine. Finally, I started to feel alive. I arrived in Tirana, got into the car the festival had sent for me, and went to the hotel. Due to the damned traffic and all the preparations in the room, I had only twenty minutes before I rushed across the city to a live TV broadcast.

After the broadcast, they immediately drove me to the National Museum, where the festival's official opening was to take place. Backstage, I was introduced to the mayor of Tirana, and we exchanged some ceremonial phrases about support and gratitude. Then, I read some poetry, and right there, without leaving the stage, I participated in a discussion about war and culture—the Balkan participants also had much to say on the topic. While sitting on stage, I felt like I was fading away, that I was disappearing, but I kept my composure and even managed to respond to questions reasonably. As one of the organizers later said, I looked so exhausted and drained that my very appearance became the best representation of the life of a Ukrainian during the war.

Despite my outward exhaustion, I still felt a bit of fire within me. So, I didn't refuse when I was invited to the Ukrainian embassy to symbolically read a few lines of Shevchenko for the Albanian establishment. At the embassy, there were several dozen MPs, businessmen, journalists, and representatives of the creative intelligentsia. There were also two ministers from the current Albanian government, who, after an hour of official ceremonies at the embassy, invited me—the only Ukrainian representative at the festival—to have tea with the second most powerful person in the country, the Speaker of the parliament. As a person, I should have apologized, explained, and refused, but as a Ukrainian, I didn't have that right. I had to work; that's why I went there in the first place

Several dozen people gathered in the Speaker's office. The atmosphere was very pleasant and relaxed; we drank tea and talked about Ukraine. With her invitation, the Speaker of the parliament, who also could have been doing her own business or resting, wanted to show her respect for Ukraine and the heroic efforts of the Ukrainian people. By being there, I wanted to express my gratitude on behalf of Ukrainians to the Albanian state—a NATO member!—and to the Albanian people for their unwavering support.

When Albanian honey was offered on a small plate with my tea, I smiled. Just the day before, I had been treated to tea and honey by a hospitable Roma family in eastern Slovakia.

Over the course of a day, I arrived from Donbas, painted a bus for the military with children, crossed the border, bought three cars for the Armed Forces of Ukraine, had tea with the Roma, inspected an ambulance, flew to Vienna, slept in secret in an airport bathroom, flew to Tirana, went on live TV, performed at the festival, and spoke with half of the Albanian government...

This is what a typical day in the life of a Ukrainian volunteer looks like—like a dizzying dream, one that could only unfold in the restroom of a far-off airport.

Techyk

As the Ukrainian proverb goes, "An old horse doesn't plow deep, but it doesn't spoil the furrows either." In today's wartime conditions, it feels like this describes the trusty old Volkswagen T4 van, or *techyk*, as Ukrainians affectionately call it. Now, with the number of vehicles I've purchased for the military having long surpassed two hundred, I can confidently say that the most common request from soldiers is the *techyk*. A pickup truck, the ideal off-road vehicle for combat zones, delivering ammunition, and evacuating the wounded, comes only in second place. And here's why.

The *techyk* is an old vehicle, but in this case, old means tried and true quality. Volkswagen produced the T4 model from 1990 to 2003 before discontinuing it and launching the next generation. The newer generations—T5, T6, and now T7—are more comfortable, advanced, and equipped with features that make driving easier and smoother. However, when it comes to reliability, they can't hold a candle to the legendary *techyk*. Any mechanic will tell you it's better to buy two old T4s than one new T5.

The advantage of this vehicle is that it comes from an era that was essentially pre-electronic. It doesn't have a powerful onboard computer or dozens of sensors; it's pure mechanics in its simplest, most elegant form. And when there are no fancy features, there's less to break. As a result, this van can be repaired with basic tools right in the field—or, in our case, on the battlefield. It's like a small tractor with a simple, logical design, free of unnecessary complexity. They say you can even pour sunflower oil into a *techyk*'s engine—it's that straightforward—and it will still run.

To back up these words, let me share a story from my own experience. During my first trip to Donbas in April 2022, some acquaintances asked me to deliver a *techyk* for scouts to Kostiantynivka as part of our convoy. We set off from Uzhhorod in the evening. About one hundred kilometers out of the city, the road begins to climb into the Carpathian Mountains before descending into Galicia after the pass. This mountain pass, with its steepest incline near the village of Abranka, serves as an important test for us. If the vehicles can handle the strain of climbing uphill at speed, they'll manage the thousand kilometers to Donbas without issue.

That *techyk* didn't pass the Abranka test. About halfway up the incline, it started sputtering and releasing thick, billowing white clouds. At first, I thought it was smoke and that the vehicle was about to catch fire, but it turned out to be steam—the radiator had overheated. The spring night in the mountains was still freezing, and in the subzero temperatures, those clouds of steam looked incredibly dramatic, like something out of a blockbuster movie.

We pulled over to the side of the road, and our mechanic, Ivan, began inspecting the vehicle. It was past midnight, everything was deserted, and there was no way to find spare parts or tools until morning. After assessing the situation, Ivan suddenly disappeared. It turned out he had wandered into the nearby woods. We thought he'd gone to relieve himself, but he returned with a "spare part"—a tree branch. Ivan took a knife, carved a plug out of the wood, and used it to block off the heater circuit. He topped up the radiator with cold water, and within ten minutes, we were back on the road. Later, everything was properly repaired at a service station, but we had witnessed a miracle: a *techyk* loaded to the roof managed to travel another thousand kilometers with a wooden spare part. After that experience, I became a devoted follower of the *techyk*, the god of war.

I bought dozens of such vehicles for the army, including passenger versions that carry up to nine people—basically a whole combat unit—cargo versions that easily carry a ton of weight, and chassis versions that can transport oversized items. With a powerful diesel engine—either 2.4 or 2.5—these vehicles perform miracles; they are real workhorses, the ants of the army. Moreover, the front-wheel drive is so reliable that with fresh tires—especially grip tires designed for traction—this vehicle can pull itself out of mud and swamps just as effectively as an all-wheel drive.

There's one more big plus—the price. Since it's an old vehicle, it's practically considered ready for disposal abroad, but the engine has a huge lifespan. So, as long as the body isn't rusted through, a *techyk* can still run for many more hundreds of thousands of kilometers in Ukraine. Cheap, tough, and reliable—that's the *techyk*!

Hose

I don't know if this will be a story about the everyday life of wartime or about my childhood. It just so happens that everything intertwines, connecting the present with the past. Events link together, pulling something completely unexpected, forgotten, and seemingly insignificant from memory—yet, at the same time, so important. Like, for example, a simple hose.

It was early June 2022. The day before, Russia had bombed all of Ukraine's oil refineries and large fuel storage facilities. The goal was simple: to stop Ukrainian military vehicles, which consume incredible amounts of diesel, and to paralyze any economic activity in the country. At one point, it seemed the enemy had at least partially achieved their goal, because gas stations were empty, and you could only get your 10 liters of fuel after waiting in line for hours. I won't even mention the price of this scarce commodity.

I remember one particular incident from that time. Our convoy, heading to the front, stopped at a WOG gas station on the bypass road in Uman. There, you could buy drinks, snacks, air fresheners, kids' toys, magazines, chewing gum—even hot oatmeal, pizza, hot dogs, burgers, cheesecake, and bottles of high-quality imported wine or whiskey. The employee summed it all up with a smile: "At our gas station, you can buy everything except fuel." That was the state of affairs back then.

We had to transport two brand new ambulances from the Committee of Medical Assistance in Transcarpathia to frontline hospitals in the Kharkiv region. There was absolutely no fuel at the gas stations; even cars had stopped pulling in.

It looked like a scene from the future: vehicles had switched to electric or some other type of charge, and gas stations had become relics, museum exhibits—like phone booths with landlines on the streets.

In Uzhhorod, with great effort and after shaking hands with ten people, you could get some diesel, as the city was located on the border with the EU, where fuel had started being imported quickly. And our magical password, "It's for the East," would open all doors and mobilize people to help. In the end, we managed to fill up the tanks completely and gather two hundred liters of diesel for the road. We poured it into a huge dirty barrel that had once contained motor oil and placed it inside the ambulance—so new that everything inside was still wrapped in plastic. Then we set out on our way.

We set off to Kharkiv in two ambulances on a 1300-kilometer journey. Passing empty gas stations along the road, we silently thanked our luck for the barrel that was traveling with us, giving us a sense of confident optimism: we would make it! A few times, when stopping at gas stations to buy water or coffee, we asked about fuel—maybe there was a special quota for emergency vehicles, for ambulances? But it was always a dead end.

Then, somewhere past Zhytomyr, the fuel reserve warning lights on both our ambulances almost simultaneously lit up. We pulled over to the side of the road and started uncapping the barrel. We slid open the window, and I lowered a long rubber hose into the barrel, stood by the tank, and got ready. First, I blew into the hose to check the connection—and the barrel bubbled cheerfully. It reminded me of when my daughter blows through a straw to make bubbles in her juice.

Then came the most unpleasant moment. I tensed up and started siphoning the diesel from the barrel—within a few seconds, a stream of diesel filled my mouth. I quickly pulled the hose out and shoved it into the tank, then turned away and spat out the diesel, sticking out my tongue like a dog in the hot summer heat. Everyone around me burst out laughing.

At that moment, my grandfather came to mind, particularly how he would go down into the cool cellar, sit on a wooden stool by an old wine barrel, prepare a glass jug lined with vine branches, and pull out a thin hose. The barrel held wine he had made himself, and it was no coincidence we lived in a town called Vynohradiv. The wine was made from Isabella grapes, a variety that sommeliers call a "grape weed," but due to its hardiness, this vine became very popular in Transcarpathian households.

Grandfather Stepan would take the hose, siphon the wine, and spit it out the first few times to clear the sediment. When the trickle became clear, he would fill the ruby drink into the jug. Having seen this process once, I decided to repeat it when the adults were not around. I took the hose, approached the barrel, siphoned the wine, and got a mouthful of sour and unpleasant drink. I was five years old, and the year was 1992. I remember that time well because that's when I first quit smoking. After spitting out that swill, I didn't drink wine for another ten years, and would never have believed that someday this particular drink—albeit not made from Isabella grapes—would become my favorite.

And then, exactly thirty years later, in the heat of the first summer of the war, standing on the side of a road somewhere between Zhytomyr and Kyiv, siphoning precious diesel from a barrel, I suddenly remembered my grandfather and the coolness of our cellar. Would he have believed that, as a child who survived war himself, I would one day be driving ambulances to positions near the Russian border, studying engine types, and learning how to spit fuel through my teeth?

It was a poignant, even tender memory. I thought to myself that life always comes full circle—it doesn't repeat exactly, although it spirals, bringing back past decades, forgotten experiences, and people who are no longer with us. The past is an echo, a resonance that responds in us today under the most unexpected circumstances.

And as for the fuel? Everything was fine. We happily made it to Kharkiv, and within a few weeks, Ukraine had fully restored its supplies and reopened gas stations across the country. Russia's plan failed, and we repelled that attack. As we did all the others, including the brutal winter attack on our energy infrastructure.

Who knows how I'll remember that first June of the war decades from now? Perhaps it will be the taste of diesel in my mouth. Or perhaps it will be the hunched figure of my grandfather, a child of war, filling a jug with homemade wine in the dimness of our cool cellar.

Khrestyshche

Krestyshche was the first village in Donbas that I visited in the spring of 2022. It was the destination for the Transcarpathian Territorial Defense, so several of my friends ended up in that village. This was a time when everything was highly classified, so the exact location was sent to us via a secure messenger just an hour before our meeting. Before that, we were traveling blindly—just heading toward Donetsk region, with more specific directions to follow once we reached Sloviansk. And that's exactly how it happened.

The village is situated between Sloviansk and Izium, near the Sviatohirsk Lavra. There are many forests and lakes around, and the area is generally beautiful, completely unlike the industrial landscape most associate with Donbas. Even the locals pointed this out, constantly correcting us: you haven't arrived in Donbas, but in Slobozhanshchyna! This is the historical territory of free people, free settlements—*slobodas*—that were established here during the Cossack era. So, administratively, it's part of Donetsk oblast, but in reality, everything around Kramatorsk is Slobozhanshchyna.

I'm not sure if they spoke this way before 2014, but at least after the war began that year, when I first started traveling to the frontline areas for literary events, this perspective was widespread. Back then, no one wanted to be identified with Donbas; people were searching for their roots elsewhere, in a different history and mythology. Interestingly, around that time in Kramatorsk and Bakhmut, I was often told that the dividing line between the occupied territories and those under the Ukrainian flag was clear: the industrial Donbas was occu-

pied, while the lands of historical agrarian Slobozhanshchyna, with their Cossack roots, remained free.

The very name—Krestyshche—also points to the ancient, Cossack origins of the village. Sources claim it was a guard post at the boundary between settled land and the barbarian steppe. This is a historical frontier territory, a line which separated civilizations—settled agricultural life from the nomadic. Somewhere along this path, where the salt traders (*chumaks*) would bring salt to the north, a cross was first erected, and later a village formed around it. Krestyshche.

On that first visit, I didn't know anything about it. We left Sloviansk, passed the checkpoint, and headed down the road through a pine forest. Up ahead, the sounds of gunfire and explosions marked the front line—there, in the direction of Izium, the territories were occupied by Russia. The GPS directed us left, toward a village situated on the border between farmland and forest. A road sign read: "Khrestyshche." That's when I learned the name of the village. It was strange to see informational signs like that; in central and western Ukraine, they had already been removed to confuse the occupiers. But here, near the front line, no one had time for such petty things, so the sign remained.

We could have died under that sign. As soon as we saw it, we decided to stop and take a photo for the memory. After all, this was our first trip to the front lines of Donbas, we were green and inexperienced, and our emotions were running high. We parked the convoy on the side of the road and lined up for the photo. Later, our commander nearly had a heart attack when he heard what we'd done. He explained that all the roadside areas were mined, and we could only move along the central part of the road. Well, we were just lucky that time.

The meeting with the military took place in a grain hangar. Under the roof, we could hide our vehicles and groups of people from enemy aerial reconnaissance. Somewhere nearby, there was constant thudding in the background, but the soldiers didn't react—they were already used to the relentless artillery fire and could tell the proximity of shell explosions by ear. In Khrestyshche, our troops had set up camp, with their positions and trenches located several kilometers away in the fields and forests. To go there daily—delivering shifts, water, food, ammunition, and building materials for bunkers—they needed the jeep we had brought.

On the outside, the village looked normal: houses, slanted fences, gardens and fields, even cows grazing. But there were very few civilians. Every now and then, military vehicles sped down the empty streets at high speed. Everyone tried to camouflage themselves and avoid drawing attention. At night, there was a light-masking regime. Phones were to be used very briefly, then switched to airplane mode to avoid revealing the number of active subscribers in the area.

The village shop was open, but they didn't sell anything fresh—only packaged goods and cigarettes. Later, an enemy rocket hit near the shop, creating a deep crater that filled with water. Over time, shelling—mostly blind, but sometimes targeted—became a routine occurrence. The only civilians left were the elderly and those often referred to as "socially unfit." Unfortunately, there were many children among them, growing up to the sound of explosions.

The soldiers lived in abandoned houses, some even doing cosmetic repairs, setting up outdoor showers, and installing new toilets. I saw with my own eyes vegetable beds with fresh produce: the military unit supplied grains, meat, and canned goods, but nothing fresh was brought in, so the soldiers planted onions and dill. New trenches were dug just behind the vegetable beds; it was the second line of defense. With each passing month, the number of homes destroyed by bombings in the village increased, yards became overgrown with tall weeds, and houses with boarded-up windows gave off a ghostly impression.

I visited Khrestyshche several times throughout the year, sometimes even spending the night with the soldiers. During this time, I got to know the village, its streets, and key landmarks a little better. Now, whenever I drive along the Izium highway through Donbas, I always turn my head melancholically in that direction. Our military has long since left, but Khrestyshche has forever become a part of my biography.

Like several villages in Kharkiv, Mykolaiv, Kherson, and Zaporizhzhia regions, where my team and I often go, where we share a table with the soldiers and sleep beside them. Many of those soldiers are no longer alive, and only memories remain, along with low-quality photos and dots on the map. Once we win, I will definitely return to these places. To take a quiet stroll and lay some flowers . . .

Baptists

———

It happened during my first trip to Donbas at the end of April 2022. Ukraine was fully embroiled in war but gripped by the uncertainty of what was to come—it was already clear by then that the Russians would not succeed in occupying the entirety of the country, but nobody knew when and how this horror would end. We purchased a pickup truck and a jeep for the military in Donbas, my second and third vehicles for the armed forces. Our friends from the medical aid committee lent us a minibus to return from Donetsk oblast; we took another car for the military from other volunteers and rallied eight drivers—two for each car so that we could take turns on the road and not waste time at rest stops. And off we went to the east.

It was my first trip, and my emotions were running high. Adrenaline was competing with fear because we were traveling from the westernmost point of Ukraine, where missiles could not reach, to Donetsk oblast, which, according to the news reports, was constantly under fire. At the time, this journey seemed extremely dangerous, plus we didn't have bulletproof vests or helmets. There was still a shortage of ammunition in the country because everything had been sent to the soldiers.

Vasyl Yuriyovych, a local government representative who had been delivering volunteer aid to the front since 2014, was traveling with us. He knew everything, and his calm and positive attitude dispelled any fears that I had. I realized the value of having such an individual on the team, and when arranging future trips, I began to prioritize drivers not only for their driving skills but also with an eye toward fostering a harmonious psychological dynamic. Each member's personality would fulfill a specific role within the team, ensuring that one person complemented or balanced another.

We left Uzhhorod at three in the morning, and the plan was simple: to cover as much distance as possible that day. Vasyl Yuriyovych said that wherever we ended up, he would arrange a place to stay for the night because it was forbidden to move around during the curfew. I naively believed that he would book something on the go through Booking.com, but it turned out that he had his own network for accommodation and assistance when traveling. That's because he is a Baptist.

I must admit that I was quite surprised that Vasyl was so casual when it came to arranging a place for us to stay. He was in no hurry to call and make arrangements—he just kept reassuring me that we would find a place to spend the night wherever the curfew found us. I had already resigned myself to the fact that it would catch us in the field, and we would spend the night in our cars. Ultimately, as the following trips showed, this was not the worst option.

As we neared Kryvyi Rih, the clock started ticking closer to curfew. Vasyl Yuriiovych searched for something on his phone, dialed a number, and informed the recipient that we were en route with a group of eight approaching soon. He then inquired, "Can we come over?" As far as I understood from the conversation, it was the first time he had ever spoken to the person on the other end of the phone. Well, well, what a good organizer we have, I thought to myself.

But a miracle happened, and twenty minutes later, we were driving through Kryvyi Rih, headed to the address we had been given. The city was drowning in darkness, as a blackout regime was implemented at night to prevent aerial attacks. We drove beside a long factory wall until we came to a courtyard in front of a three-story building. It was the Baptist community center in Kryvyi Rih, and it was located next door to ArcelorMittal Kryvyi Rih. The industrial giant is the No. 1 target for attacks in this city, so it seemed crazy to spend the night next to it. As soon as the door to the Baptist community center opened, an air raid siren went off nearby. Trust me, the air raid sirens in Uzhhorod and Kryvyi Rih may sound identical, but they evoke entirely different feelings. My body trembled at the sound.

Disregarding the unsettling sound of the buzzer, a middle-aged man with a beard ushered us inside. He showed us the sinks and toilets, as well as a room with mattresses lying on the floor in long rows. Then he went to the kitchen to make tea and prepare a snack. This house had become a shelter for many people over the past two months, most of them refugees fleeing the occupied south and Donbas.

For some, this house served as a temporary stop on the way westward, while others settled here for a longer period of time, hoping that the occupation of their homeland would soon come to an end. Needless to say, in a house where many different people gathered, ranging from the elderly and the disabled to babies and young adults, it was not always clean, and it did not always smell good. It's hard for a room housing fifty people sleeping close together, with windows taped to prevent shattering during explosions and carefully curtained to avoid attracting enemy aircraft, to smell fresh. But at the same time, there was some kind of comfort, a sense of security, and—strange as it may seem—home in that place. It was a home for people without a home.

Having washed ourselves, we headed to the kitchen. There was a warm meal on the table, and we pulled out some of our own provisions from our backpacks. Suddenly, the owner of the house invited us to pray. I lowered my head and listened. They prayed in their own words. They were simply thanking God for giving us this food and shelter, for giving us a chance to meet these people, asking for a safe night and an easy journey tomorrow, for protection for our soldiers and care for our people and peace. It was short and to the point. As an atheist, I even liked it. Though perhaps I was just so tired that I didn't have the energy for some of my typical biting jokes about the church as a business.

The air raid alert seemed to last all night, but we fell into a groggy sleep and paid no attention to anything. In the morning, we got up, washed ourselves, prayed (I should have used a sarcastic smiley face emoji here), had a snack, and continued on our way to Donbas. It was my first direct experience of communicating with Baptists.

There were dozens more of these experiences over the next year. There is a beautiful farm near Uzhhorod, and it is run by the local Baptist community, where we often receive large loads of fresh fruit and vegetables, other food, and various humanitarian aid to take in our jeeps to the east and pass it on to people in dire need.

We often stayed at a Baptist shelter in Pavlohrad, a city situated along the Dnipro-Donetsk highway. In fact, it is the gateway to Donbas, the last relatively peaceful city at the entrance to hell. We spent the night there before going to the front. Our hostess, an elderly lady named Dina, provided us with a hot meal, a warm shower, and a clean bed no matter when we arrived. I witnessed the continuous influx of refugees seeking shelter there and observed the regular flow of people coming to the church annex every morning for free food packages.

What I witnessed altered my perspective, transforming my flippant attitude toward religion and God. No, I didn't become a believer or join any religious denomination, but these days, I don't allow myself to make jokes about religion anymore. I am an atheist, and I have my own superficial vision of all these theological issues, but now I understand how important and formative religion is for society and how useful and effective it can be for communities, especially in times of devastating upheaval.

This isn't about the Baptists but about religious communities in general. During the war, I witnessed firsthand how religion can truly assist people. Take, for instance, the Greek Catholic priest who conducts services at a Rotonda church near Uzhhorod. He mobilized his small community to aid refugees, providing shelter and sustenance to hundreds fleeing the war as they passed through Uzhhorod on their way to the European Union. Similarly, Jewish rabbis orchestrated evacuations from war zones while simultaneously delivering humanitarian aid to Ukraine. Then there's the Islamic mufti who served as a chaplain in the army, effectively functioning as a psychologist for Crimean Tatars who volunteered for the war effort. These instances illustrated to me, for the first time, how religion can truly be a service to people.

This experience was truly transformative for me. It shifted my worldview, prompting personal growth and marking the end of my youthful frivolity. It taught me to refrain from mocking the faithful and their leaders, restoring the respect for these individuals that I had lost at the age of twelve when I first read *Thus Spoke Zarathustra*.

This story, this example, is important to me because it demonstrates how, in times of war, seemingly banal things take on their true meaning again. We are witnessing how the state has become effective, how civil society has really emerged, united, and lent a shoulder to the same state it had previously kept a distance from and against which it had nurtured a traditional postcommunist distrust. Institutions began to work, and simple professions regained their importance and respect.

The war became a point of reset for the entire state, filling old sacs with new content. For decades after the fall of the Soviet Union, a bizarre, painful, perverse reality with shifted values and social orientations was being created in Ukraine. Success was equated with quick wealth, and access to it was gained through joining the government or engaging in corruption scams. A good illustration of this is the fact that for a good twenty years after independence, the most popular university majors in Ukraine were law and economics, although it was the rule of law and economics that we had the biggest problems with.

However, there was also a growing desire for change in society, as evidenced by the Orange Revolution of 2004-2005 and the Revolution of Dignity of 2013-2014. The war greatly accelerated the healing process, and it turned out that the Security Service could protect the state and catch enemy agents, not just create headaches for businesses. It became evident that during critical moments, officials at the highest levels of government and local self-governance can prioritize serving the state and its citizens rather than solely focusing on their own interests and those of their inner circle. This principle applies across various spheres of society.

I remember how, in the first days of the war, I was loading humanitarian aid onto trains that were headed from Uzhhorod to Kharkiv and how the conductors of these trains were under fire. They did it for their usual minuscule salary when they could have just quit and refused to work, but they continued doing so because it was their professional duty. For this daily feat, all Ukrzaliznytsia employees have earned incredible respect from Ukrainians.

I remember how, in early June 2022, my team and I spent the night in Kharkiv. There was an air raid alert and missile strikes in the city center. Since it was a curfew, we decided to stop by before leaving at six in the morning to see the aftermath of the enemy shelling. Imagine our surprise when we saw that the utility workers had already cleaned up almost everything and were sweeping up the remaining debris! They could have run away, quit, or refused to work under such conditions for the minimum wage, but they stayed because that was their role in this war. They resisted Russian terror by cleaning and restoring order, pushing back chaos and horror. And they did it with such dignity!

There are also the electricians who spent the entire autumn and winter of 2022-23 under fire, trying to restore critical infrastructure for people in the rain and snow as quickly as possible. Electricians are heroes, although who could have said before that the electrician's profession is heroic and people would be ready to kiss their hands and thank them for their work?

And so on and so forth: a doctor, a firefighter, a postal bus driver, a teacher who went out to her classroom under fire to give children the illusion of safety and normalcy, gas station attendants who stood at their workplace on the Zhytomyr highway without a break during the first three days of the war to refuel the cars of people fleeing occupation to the west, even though any gas station could explode at any moment from a gunshot or shell. In those early days, nobody knew whether they would be paid at the end of the month, whether the hryvnia would still be in circulation, or whether the state would still exist. And yet they stood there and did their heroic work anyway...

That's how everything reverted to basics during the war—professions and social roles regained significance and earned respect from society. Now, we no longer say, "I love my country, but not the state," because we feel that this state is ours. Now, it is not a shame to be a janitor, but dignified. Being a priest in the twenty-first century is not worthy of snarky jokes. Doing good to others is not trivial.

All that was rotten and weak, which was crippled by the postcommunist transformation, has woken up and got back on its feet, filled with meaning. There was a great restart of the state and social ties, new models of success and respect. And it is this great restart that fills me with faith in a better future for us and our country. That's how I got my faith...

Air raid in Bakhmut

Each air raid siren is unique and unmistakable. They sound different by day and night, in winter and summer, and take on a different tone depending on the geographical coordinates and the device triggering the alarm.

Late evening, winter 2023, curfew in Kharkiv. I'm staying in a hotel after a literary event in the city. The hotel has a shelter, but the receptionist, when I checked in, said that only foreigners go down there. I paused for a moment—was she saying this with approval or with a mocking judgment? I'm reading a book when I hear muffled explosions somewhere in the city, look out the window, and see a glow from the blasts. The explosions continue, the night sky lit up by a meteor shower of sparks and shrapnel. I check the news in the local media and learn that they hit a fireworks warehouse, which explains the many "fireworks" in the sky. I text my wife, saying everything's fine, I'm alive. Only after that does the air raid siren go off in Kharkiv—for cities near the Russian border or the front line, missiles arrive faster than the air raid siren.

Autumn 2022, morning, Uzhhorod. I've just dropped my daughter off at kindergarten and returned home to take a shower. Outside the window, the air raid siren starts wailing. I curse and get ready to go back: I need to pick up my daughter, because during air raids, they take the little ones to the bomb shelter—a damp, old basement that smells of mildew and potatoes. If an air raid sounds during nap time, they still wake the kids up and take them to the basement—that's the protocol. Although pretty much everyone in Uzhhorod is confident that a missile will never reach us, since it's a city on the border with the EU. I don't have such illusions, so whenever possible, I always pick my child up from kindergarten—better to have her with me.

Summer 2023, late evening, Uzhhorod. I'm reading a fairy tale to my daughter, listening to her breathing, hoping she'll finally calm down and fall asleep. Through the open window, the sound of the air raid siren drifts in. My heartbeat automatically quickens. My child flinches, and sleep escapes her. She starts babbling something about "sywen" and "wockets"—that's the vocabulary of a two-year-old Ukrainian child.

May 2022, Bakhmut, midday. We've brought a pickup truck and a heap of various useful things, from bulletproof vests to sleeping bags and energy drinks. There are seven of us and about a dozen soldiers. We talk, laugh, ask about the battles around Popasna, and inquire about the experience of friends who, just three months ago, were actors in a theater, and now stand before us with rifles. The air raid siren sounds—and immediately, there's no one around. A pile of things sits on the asphalt, with us volunteers standing around it, and the soldiers are gone. After the siren sounded, they scattered: some have rushed off in the pickup truck, away from the buildings, others ran to grab helmets and bulletproof vests, while the rest hid in the underground shelter. I'm in shock because I've never seen such a swift and clear reaction to the siren. In Uzhhorod, by the third month of the war, no one even stops drinking coffee on the terraces of cafes when that sound is heard. It turns out that the air raid siren in Bakhmut and the air raid siren in Uzhhorod are two very different things . . .

Early July 2022, Berlin, on an S-Bahn train. I'm heading to my first international appearance since the full-scale invasion began, trying to organize my main talking points in my head. There's so much I want to say to the Germans, but there won't be much time during the panel. Suddenly, my phone in my pocket starts howling—there's an air raid alert in my hometown. A wave of fear hits me because my wife and child are there alone, while I'm here in Berlin, seemingly for no good reason. A panic attack sets in: I feel like this time—by the law of misfortune—a missile is bound to hit Uzhhorod. With trembling hands, I grab my phone, trying to turn off the alarm app and text my wife; Berliners glare at me with irritation because I'm disrupting their peace. I feel ashamed that we're being killed. It's surreal.

Summer 2023, Zaporizhzhia, night. We're returning from the southern front, heading back to Uzhhorod. We have a document that theoretically allows us to travel during curfew across the entire territory of Ukraine, but this time it's disregarded, and we're forced to stop and sleep right at the checkpoint. The reason is that we need to cross a bridge over the Dnipro River, which is essentially the dam of the DniproHES. There's a high likelihood that the Russians, who have recently destroyed the Kakhovka HPP dam, will target this one with their missiles. If that happens, we could end up buried under the rubble.

But there's also the peculiar possibility that we have a front-row seat to a harrowing sight, something we'll remember for the rest of our lives. I even jot down an idea for an essay about *ruinomania*—a peculiar psychological disorder where, during war, a person automatically imagines everything they see around them as destroyed and burned. A sort of pastime for the mentally unwell.

Someday, after the war, we'll have the final statistics on air raid alerts. Hundreds and thousands of siren sounds, locations of strikes, casualty numbers. We'll know the exact number of hours we spent under air raid alerts over these years. We'll recall some of them in vivid detail. We'll ask friends twenty years from now: "What were you doing during that particular air raid?"

For me, personally, it will also be a private tally of how many times I've uttered the phrase, "Let them die." Because every time I hear a siren, I send that wish into the universe. I hope it will be heard.

On the road

I want to write all of this in one endless sentence because its
 perfect rhyme is the road—a long asphalt path stretching
 somewhere to disappear beyond the horizon, to vanish
 around the bend, to beckon forward;
because driving is the best part of our work; you can't
 understand Ukraine from the sky; it's hard to feel it from
 the sleeping car of a train; you have to drive across Ukraine,
this vast country, the largest on the continent,
because Ukraine is the America of Europe;
taste it by diving inside of a car speeding from the west to the
 east, then from the east back to the west; savor the highs of
 the road,
these 1,500 kilometers, a day and a half without sleep
 or rest through mountains and passes, villages and
 towns, winding bypasses of regional centers, fields and
 windbreaks, shady forests and ravines;
emerge onto the open steppe to feel like a grain of sand
 carried by the wind,
a tumbleweed fed by the road, by distances, by the changing
 landscapes;
the road is a drug you quickly grow addicted to,
repeating the route, you conquer it, knowing its curves and
 dips by heart—it's like caressing a lover's body, every
 centimeter scanned by your fingertips, kissed and warmed;
driving from Uzhhorod to Donbas is greeting the dawn
 on the road, when the sun rises directly in front of your
 windshield, exactly where it's meant to rise, in the east,
 toward which you're moving;

its pink glow slowly envelopes the twilight before bursting
 triumphantly and refracting its full palette of colors
 through the glass;
you roll down the window slightly, letting in fresh air to begin
 a new day,
when you've been awake for over a day and the hum of the
 wheels feels like a natural background sound;
your consciousness suddenly opens a narrow door, letting
 your mind absorb the road,
it maps the contours of the terrain onto your soul, making
 you a part of this space
and this space a part of you;
you don't need any chemical substances, no potions, no
 shamanic brews—just stay awake and keep driving,
 swapping night for day;
just listen to the music and the creak of rubber against
 asphalt, let the engine respond to every shift in your mood
 and biorhythm;
and then, at some moment, enlightenment will come—the
 road will seep into your lower back. you'll feel it rising
 along your spine, snaking its way through each vertebra,
 slithering like a sly serpent into your brain,
and the flash of dawn, this light from the east,
will consume you; surrender to it, let go of your ego, drive
 and savor it; spend long hours alone with your thoughts
 and memories;
the road is a kind of confession,
travel it to the end and, without signaling,
take a sharp turn, step on the gas,
unleashing all the horsepower trapped in those magical pipes
 and tubes,
those boiling alchemical flasks and injectors; harness that
 power
to keep moving forward, never making a full stop.

The story I will never write

———

Unfortunately, during the war, there's neither time, opportunity, nor energy to write fiction. Yet ideas for stories emerge in my mind almost daily. I often encounter prototypes for rich, vibrant characters, and both fantastical and realistic plots seem to form themselves in my thoughts, as if struggling to escape the painful daily reality.

One such unwritten work could have been a short story about a middle-aged woman working on the Slovak side of the Ukrainian-Slovak border. She sits in a temporary settlement adorned with large UN logos, and her job is to welcome Ukrainians who have just crossed the border, stepping into the safety of the EU.

Right there, just beyond the barbed wire fence separating the world of war from the world of safety and abundance, Ukrainians are supposed to receive their first assistance from her—advice, logistical and legal tips, guidance on obtaining refugee status, but also warmth, a snack, and coffee. All of this happens under the auspices of the UN, as proudly announced by a glowing neon sign. Aid to those in need in its purest form.

The story already seems to be taking perfect shape. But then, another character enters the scene—a Ukrainian writer who, during the war, has been compelled to take on the role of a volunteer supporting the army.

It's ten in the morning, October, the first cold days of autumn. The writer shows up at the border on the Ukrainian side. Because he's a man, he faces a long and thorough check. Ukrainian men are prohibited from leaving the country during the war, with one of the few exceptions being volunteer work delivering humanitarian aid.

So, the writer spends a good hour and a half at the border while polite border guards carefully check and scan his documents, verifying his right to leave with their superiors.

A few words about the setting: it's a typical Central European border, a pedestrian crossing between a Ukrainian and a Slovak village. Typical because, in this small example, one could easily get lost in the complexities of twentieth-century history and the formation of independent Central European states.

The Central European-ness of the border lies in the fact that it's a Ukrainian-Slovak crossing, but ethnic Hungarians live on both sides of it. *A perfect topic for an essay about Central Europe*, the writer muses as he waits for his documents at the small window.

Finally, he finds himself on the Slovak side. Of course, the writer would never say "on the European side," since, to him, the EU and Europe are not the same thing—a thought he files away for that essay. But thinking is becoming increasingly difficult, as the hour-long drive to the border and an additional hour and a half at the crossing have left his body urgently signaling the need for a brief stop. *I shouldn't have drunk so much coffee and water this morning*, he concludes, just as he spots a promising UN sign ahead. *Surely, they'll help there!*

With determined steps, he enters the grounds of what is supposed to be the world's most reliable and efficient organization. To his left stands a neat portable restroom. The young man reaches for the door handle but notices a lock. This can't be! Is the restroom actually closed to visitors? Is this really how an organization with billions in its budget greets people fleeing a war-torn country?

It must be a mistake. The writer heads to the temporary UN office to ask for a key. Inside sits a middle-aged woman who doesn't speak Slovak. Judging by her accent, she's French. She looks up in surprise and shakes her head. No, the restroom isn't working. Why not? Just because. It's simply out of order. She shuts the window.

Stunned, the writer returns to the restroom and takes a picture of the lock with his phone. The woman bursts out of the warm office and asks, "What are you photographing?"

"The lock on the restroom."

"For what purpose?"

"To have a keepsake of the UN's usefulness in today's world."

"Don't," she exclaims. "I'll get you the key right now!"

But the writer has already turned and walked away. After all, he doesn't need the restroom *that* badly—he can wait. The woman watches him leave, irritated. Then she sighs, strolls back into the office, and resumes writing her letter:

> *Dear Cecile,*
>
> *Thank you so much for your letter. It's nice to know that you're interested in what's going on with me.*
>
> *As I told you three weeks ago, this assignment is necessary for me to sort out my financial matters. Since it involves working close to a country at war, the salary here includes all kinds of allowances and bonuses, so in a few months, I'll earn as much as I would have in two years in Marseille. I'm hoping the war lasts at least until the end of spring, so I can save enough to fix up our summer house in the village.*

Overall, things are going well. We've settled in and have a decent amount of work. I've been provided with an official apartment, and they even cover our meals. Plus, everything is cheap here in Slovakia, so I'm not depriving myself of anything. The people around me are better than I expected. It's, of course, the wild East, but it's livable. They're even funny and sweet in their own way.

My workplace is right by the border, but I'm completely safe since Slovakia is in the EU and NATO, and the front line in Ukraine is a thousand and a half kilometers away. Still, according to our internal regulations, this is considered a conflict zone, which is why the salary is so high. There aren't many Ukrainians here right now; there are virtually no refugees. Those who wanted to leave did so last year, so now people are crossing the border more for work than to escape the war. My day usually looks like this: I drink coffee, watch some TV show, and scroll through Instagram. It's a bit painful, of course, seeing all my friends in Marseille living a full life while I'm stuck here in the middle of nowhere. But it's nothing, it won't last long.

So, everything is good with me. The only thing is the Ukrainians sometimes get a bit annoying with their questions: if it weren't for them, this would be the perfect job.

I won't be able to send you a gift from Slovakia for Christmas because there's nothing pretty or delicious here, but I'll order something from home for you.

Hugs and I miss you, dear Cecile,
Your Charlotte
October 12, 2023, Veľké Selmenče, Slovakia

Hazelnut

This story would probably be better left unwritten, to be told in a small circle, laughed at, and immediately forgotten. But still, such an absurd, Švejk-like adventure—about our time and our war, about the truth of life—should be recorded, so that many decades from now, readers will see Ukrainian soldiers as real people, not just as marble statues of ancient gods.

It happened in the spring of 2022, during one of my first trips to the front lines. The state was just beginning to manage the logistical chaos, so the military still needed all sorts of things—from helmets to socks and pasta.

With money collected from people, I bought three jeeps and was preparing for a trip to Donbas. Relatives of the soldiers brought backpacks and boxes of personal packages for the troops, but there was still some free space left in the trunks, which we decided to fill with food. The logic was that the soldiers could either use it themselves or distribute it to the local population.

We loaded the vehicles with canned goods, pasta, grains, sweet cookies, and energy drinks, and we also added several boxes of hazelnuts. A local entrepreneur had a whole grove where he grew these tasty nuts for the confectionery industry and decided to send a little to the front. We took it and delivered it to the soldiers.

The soldiers thanked us, but two weeks later, when I was preparing to go to Donbas again and called them to ask, "What do you need? What should I bring?" they responded categorically, "Bring everything except the hazelnuts." I was surprised by such a response and the sharpness of their tone, but for some reason, no one wanted to tell me the details.

Everything became clear when we had a bit of time to talk in a more informal setting. Usually, the soldiers we visit prepare a warm lunch or dinner for us, and it's during the meal that we exchange news and gossip.

The story about the hazelnuts was that everyone liked them a lot. Perhaps too much. That was the problem. The reality of positional warfare in the spring of 2022 was that the army had dug in at their positions and were engaged in artillery duels. Ukrainian soldiers would take shifts at their positions, and depending on the section of the front, they had to sit in the trenches for at least a day. In some cases, shifts lasted up to three days because the intense enemy shelling made more frequent rotations difficult and dangerous.

And so the soldiers would sit in the trenches, ready to fend off Russian attacks. The enemy would bombard Ukrainian positions with a downpour of shells and other artillery, making it extremely unwise to leave the trench even for a minute. Therefore, the soldiers would take with them supplies of food and water for several days. For one of these shifts, the soldiers had even brought along a large box of hazelnuts.

What is there to do in a trench for several days? All the topics have been discussed, the cigarettes smoked, the books read. And then they remembered the hazelnuts—and started eating them like chips. The nuts were tasty, slightly roasted, and nutritious. Who would ever allow themselves to eat so many hazelnuts in peacetime, since they're so expensive? But here they could eat as many as they wanted!

Hazelnuts are indeed an expensive snack because they're calorie-dense and have great taste and texture. But the problem is that they are also oily, and therefore heavy on the digestive system. The soldiers ate the hazelnuts by the handful and didn't realize the consequences. Leaving out the gruesome details, they shared what happened next, but even in broad strokes, it's shocking.

First, the vomiting started. Soon after, diarrhea followed. Then, for a while, they suffered from both simultaneously. It should be noted that, in the conditions of artillery warfare, soldiers don't leave the trenches to relieve themselves. Excuse my bluntness, but they simply use plastic bags, which are tied up and tossed out of the trench with a sweeping motion, like grenades being thrown at the enemy advancing.

> They say the battlefield around that trench was littered with such "grenades."

> And in my later trips to the front, I brought the soldiers anything they needed.

> But hazelnuts—never again.

Humor that heals us

———

It's impossible to survive a war without humor. Yes, sometimes laughter can be bitter, it can be dark, and occasionally a weary smile is washed away by tears, but humor remains one of the most effective defense mechanisms for the human psyche. Think of laughter as a shock absorber, cushioning us as we navigate the deep potholes of the catastrophe of war that has come to define our daily lives.

From the first days of the full-scale invasion, humor became Ukraine's protective shield. And, as is often the case, jokes contained only a bit of wit, but mostly the truth, various cultural (often unconscious) subtexts, and countless shades of irony, satire, and sarcasm. Take the elderly woman from the southern steppes, for instance, who advised the Russian invaders to load their pockets with sunflower seeds so that, at the very least, sunflowers would sprout from their decaying corpses.

Compressed into the form of an internet meme, a good joke would become viral in a matter of minutes, gathering millions of views. It provided a way to deal with the overwhelming reality, which the mind found difficult to accept—such was the surreal and unbelievable nature of the new world we were facing. For instance, after the revelation of the terrible crimes and looting by the Russian army in Irpin, Hostomel, Bucha, and Borodi anka, a meme appeared featuring a wooden mock-up of a washing machine standing at the edge of the woods. The caption: "Hunting for live bait."

You have to be Ukrainian to burst out laughing: the occupiers were stealing washing machines, toilets, and even sneakers from Ukrainian homes on a massive scale. It was a shock to us that someone could live so poorly that they would steal such basic household items thousands of kilometers from their own home. Russian propaganda spoke of the "noble" goal of liberating Ukraine from the fascists who had ruined the country, only to reveal that the occupiers were shocked by the standard of living in Ukraine. This was the geopolitical subtext. The cultural undertone, on the other hand, referenced the idea of barbarians attacking a more sophisticated civilization. While there is room to expand these subtexts, they all began with a joke about a washing machine at the forest's edge, which ultimately evolved into a symbol of resistance—the desire to trap and defeat the invaders using clever tricks.

When the whole world feared the start of nuclear war, Ukrainians came up with a meme about Shchekavytsia. It's one of the hills in Kyiv, and that's where the jokesters suggested people gather for an orgy in the event of a deadly bomb strike. They said, if we're going to die, let's do it while making love and enjoying life. T-shirts appeared almost immediately with the slogan "I will be the first on Shchekavytsia," a massive online group was created where people not only joked, but also made arrangements for intimate meetings or exchanged explicit photos. Shchekavytsia became our response to the threat of a nuclear strike, against which neither ordinary people nor a non nuclear state can do anything. In such circumstances, when fatalism takes over—embodied by the hill of Shchekavytsia—there was nothing to do but spit in the aggressor's filthy face, crack open champagne, and laugh, savoring the final moments of life.

It's no coincidence that the foundation of modern Ukrainian culture is traced back to Ivan Kotliarevskyi's *Aeneid*. This parody of a seminal work of high literature from the Roman Empire, created by a Ukrainian during the time of the Russian Empire, serves as a sort of base, a lens through which we view the world. Of course, this humor, this worldview, was not created by Kotliarevskyi—he merely captured and reproduced one of the traits of the Ukrainian mentality in a genius way: a squinting, skeptical glance at the empire, at foreign power and violence, mocking the threat. *Aeneas was a lively young man*—this is about the modern Ukrainian soldier, who places a mock washing machine at the forest's edge to lure a bloodthirsty Russian soldier into a trap!

It is important to add that the sense of humor of Ukrainians, this witty view of themselves, their history, and the tragedies that have befallen our people, fits very naturally into the broader context of Central European humor. Aeneas here is a distant cousin of the soldier Švejk. Because what, in fact, unites Central Europe? Aside from geography, which isn't always obvious—which is why it's often referred to as Eastern Europe—and the identical railway stations in its cities, as Czech writer Bohumil Hrabal once aptly pointed out.

In my opinion, Central European psychology and culture have two main characteristics: a love for melancholy and a grim sense of humor. Melancholy, this often inexplicable sadness, is intrinsic to the Central European soul. This aura of quiet sorrow is perhaps connected to the continental climate, with its long winters and gloomy, foggy autumns.

Meanwhile, the distinctive Central European humor emerged because (or despite) of its tragic history. The history of Central European countries and peoples is one of living alongside powerful, intimidating empires, centuries of statelessness and oppression, and numerous wars in which Central Europeans were mere cannon fodder.

Central Europe could also be defined differently: it's the region with the highest concentration of catastrophes per square kilometer, a living museum of defeats and miseries. Historically speaking, when Germany fights Russia, they do so on Central European soil, destroying and burning everything in their path. And when these empires decide to conquer or occupy someone, their armies primarily threaten Central Europe.

Such a history drives a person to either the noose or, at the very least, to depression. Or to drink. As the aforementioned Hrabal once said: "Anyone who wants to live in Central Europe cannot be sober." Czechs, Hungarians, Romanians, Poles, Slovaks, Ukrainians, Croats, Jews, and other Central Europeans have lived for centuries with a sense of danger, feeling out threats, anticipating the start of a new war and occupation. If one takes such a life seriously, one could go mad. This is why they invented their own special remedy—humor.

Nobel laureate and supporter of the idea of Central Europe, Olga Tokarczuk, shares this observation about our type of humor:

> Milan Kundera explains it like this: in Franz Kafka's world, comedy doesn't create a counterpoint to tragedy, as, for example, in Shakespeare—there, comedy balances tragedy, it becomes a respite, it's cathartic. In Kafka's work, comedy is inherent to the tragic situation, it somehow mocks it from the inside.
>
> ...A large part of the world today reads Kafka as a gloomy author, and his books as frightening and depressive, perhaps reminiscent of modern horror films. But when Kafka first read the beginning of *The Trial* to his friends, everyone—including the author himself—laughed until they cried.

> How could one not laugh? In the morning, two men come to K. and arrest him. When K., in his nightshirt, tries to explain something to them, they eat his breakfast. Or: Gregor Samsa wakes up in the morning as a giant insect, but all he thinks about is how to get to the office on time and not be late for work.

This entire long introduction and theoretical part were necessary only to justify the following story. The thing is, the entire work of our volunteer team is permeated with a specific brand of dark and extremely politically incorrect humor. Undoubtedly, it's immoral, but please forgive us: when you frequently face danger and witness terrifying destruction and death, such humor becomes fitting. Especially in a team of men that has been driving to the front for several days almost without sleep and is on the brink of exhaustion. If we didn't joke—especially about each other—we would snap into aggression and conflict. Silly and disgusting jokes allow us to blow off steam and relieve tension so we can continue moving forward together.

One time, a famous soccer player, a true sports star, came with us to the southern front. Before the trip, I made sure to emphasize on social media that such a well-known person was joining us. I thanked everyone for their support and involvement. And then came the time for the prank. At that point, our trip to the military units had an additional, sad goal: we had to retrieve the personal car of our friend, who had passed away from a heart attack while on duty. His jeep had to be picked up from one of the southern coastal regions and brought to his family in Transcarpathia.

Somewhere near Uman, after we had already traveled seven hundred kilometers and there was no turning back, I gathered our whole team at a gas station and addressed the soccer player. I said, "Listen, you're a big star, and we've brought you along to help us with a difficult but noble task. Our friend in the military has passed away. Since he didn't die in battle but from natural causes, the military administration can't transport his body across the country for free. And transporting it by commercial refrigerated truck is far too expensive for his poor family. So, we've decided to bring him back ourselves in his own jeep.

"And we'll do this thanks to your fame and authority, dear soccer player. We'll take the body of the deceased and put it in the back of the jeep. You'll sit next to him, like an old friend. In the stiffened hand of the deceased soldier, we'll place a can of Pepsi, so he looks a little more lifelike. When we get stopped at checkpoints and they check our documents, you'll embrace him and say that your friend has just fallen asleep because he was on a long shift. In this way, you'll help the family of the deceased by doing a noble deed."

The drivers from our team, who had already gotten used to such pranks and humor after more than twenty trips, nodded approvingly and seriously confirmed my words. The stunned soccer player turned pale and looked around, unable to believe his own ears, but we played our parts confidently. The next day, we kept the joke going about the deceased: someone gave the soccer player dark sunglasses so he could put them on his future companion, someone else suggested recording a stranger's voice on his phone and playing it at the checkpoints, as if from the supposedly sleeping deceased: "Leave me alone, let me rest..." In short, the soccer player believed us and was already preparing for the return trip.

The prank was revealed when we finally arrived at the military unit. There, the soccer player was told that the soldier's body had been sent home without any problems at the government's expense, and all that was left was to pick up his car. After learning about our made-up story, the entire military unit laughed for a long time and even continued the tale. In their jokes, the deceased brother-in-arms was seated on a chair and supposedly stood guard at the entrance gates; there was a particularly realistic joke about how the deceased continued to receive his salary, was given uniforms and food for several months; and the more audacious ones joked that they had placed the stiff body of the deceased in the commander's chair, and for a month, no one noticed the difference—on the contrary, the work had only improved because no one was disturbing anyone.

One of the deceased's brother-in-arms summed up our prank like this: "You guys came up with a great idea, because in this way, he lived with us for a few more days, in our jokes and conversations. And since he had such a cheerful and easy-going nature, I'm sure he would have liked such a send-off from this world to the next."

Well, I hope I won't regret having written down this story. Life is what it is, and so is our humor.

Oh, and in case it isn't obvious, the soccer player never traveled with us again.

The smirk of the beast

I'm one of those who knew a larger scale war was coming. I didn't have access to any classified information, but everything around us was quickly heading toward the worst possible outcome, and it didn't take extraordinary insight to see that.

It was all happening right before our eyes, the whole world knew about it, so when the president of the United States first said he had reliable information about Putin's plan to start an aggression, and then almost all the diplomatic missions fled Kyiv, the conclusion was obvious.

However, most Ukrainians refused to believe it, rejecting the idea. Partially, they were lulled by the mantra of the Ukrainian authorities that there would be no war, but the main reason for rejecting the obvious was something else—the instinct of self-preservation. Because if you accept the fact that an invasion of a huge barbaric army is coming, along with shootings and torture, the bombing of civilian cities, destruction of strategic dams, and potentially the use of nuclear weapons, then it's better to commit suicide right away. But suicide—from a natural perspective—is not normal.

Ukrainians didn't believe in the war because of their sense of normalcy. For a mentally sound, rational person, it's almost impossible to fathom that in the twenty-first century—in the age of electric cars and Instagram—a full-scale war, civilian killings, massive tank battles, and the terror of occupation could actually happen. It's normal to believe that no one could simply wish for the death of millions.

It turns out that believing in the approaching war wasn't entirely normal. And not only did I believe, but I also prepared for it in my own way. For example, in January, I stocked up on nonperishable food, withdrew money from all my accounts, anticipating that the banking system might collapse, and prudently converted my savings into dollars and euros, fearing rapid devaluation once the fighting began.

Then I did something completely irrational: since a major war was looming, I decided to get in as much skiing as possible. After all, who knows when I'd next get a chance to relax in the mountains? I skied more frequently and intensely during the 2021/22 season than ever before. By early February, I had even planned a trip with friends to Bosnia—to the slopes of the Sarajevo '84 Winter Olympics—but those plans were thwarted by a nasty bout of COVID-19. After spending a week recovering at home, I took my wife and child to stay with my mother-in-law and headed off to Jasná, the nearest major ski resort in Slovakia.

Yes, I spent the final weekend before the full-scale war skiing in Slovakia—and I'm genuinely glad I lived life to the fullest while I still could. Even there, though, all the conversations in the ski gondolas revolved around the possibility of war in Ukraine. That Saturday, my extensive interview with *Politika*, Serbia's oldest newspaper, was published. Once again, I warned the public that war was inevitable.

And what do you think someone who's warning everyone about an impending apocalypse does? No, skiing wasn't the craziest thing I did. Returning from the slopes on Monday, I packed my bags, and on Tuesday, February 22, I headed to Kyiv. I remember buying the ticket right before the train's departure at the Uzhhorod station. I figured the war could start at any moment, making my trip pointless. There were plenty of tickets to Kyiv; the train was nearly empty. In contrast, trains heading in the opposite direction were completely packed. People were already leaving the capital in droves, but I was heading straight there—even though I'd been shouting across half of Europe, "Hey, there's going to be a war!"

That Wednesday before the start of the full-scale war, I enjoyed my last peaceful day and the beauty of a frosty February city. I woke at dawn on Thursday to the sound of explosions. Now you can understand why calling me normal probably isn't accurate.

I need to clarify something: I had no doubt that there would be a war, but I couldn't imagine it would be so deadly and horrifying. I thought there would be an offensive from Crimea and Donbas, an attempt to create a stillborn Novorossiya. But even in my worst nightmares, I couldn't envision an attempt to seize Kyiv, missile strikes on Lutsk, Lviv, and Ivano-Frankivsk in the very first hours, or an effort to annihilate the Ukrainian state itself. I never imagined that kill lists would become our reality.

There was only one moment when my rationality switched off and something deep inside me screamed in fear. It happened on the evening of Monday, February 21, 2022. I had returned from Slovakia, was making myself a snack in the kitchen at home, and, while preparing for another interview, watched Putin's video address recognizing the independence of the so-called Donetsk and Luhansk People's Republics. The speech itself was aggressive and delusional, as is always the case with that little tyrant, but one detail sent a chill down my spine. At first, it felt like a wave of heat, then cold. It was as if an earthquake was about to strike. My heart raced, my teeth clenched. A panic attack that lasted for just one second. It felt as though I had glimpsed the underworld.

It happened at the end of Putin's address, when he said Ukraine would soon experience "real decommunization" and smirked slyly. He knew he would attack in two days—and he was savoring the moment. A maniac looking at his victim, relishing their future suffering. In that—there's no other way to put it—smirk, for a moment, the snarl of a beast emerged. It was the maw of death, ready to seize life and drag it into its cold otherworld.

In that instant, I saw the embodiment of pure evil. A concentration of malevolent energy that has appeared in various corners of the planet for thousands of years, sowing death and chaos. I saw it and was horrified.

I never told anyone about this because it felt shameful to speak of such things—I'm not some village grandmother imagining evil spirits. But within forty hours, it became clear I hadn't been mistaken: it was planetary evil in its purest form. And it wasn't us looking at it—it was greedily leering at us.

A moment of truth

I've been watching videos from across Ukraine, and I can't shake a sense of déjà vu.

It's as if I've seen these people somewhere before, as if I recognize their facial features, their profiles, their distinct expressions. My God, it feels like something ancient has awakened and is speaking through us.

These are our archetypal images come to life: the princely warriors, Cossack armies, defenders of the Ukrainian People's Republic, and UPA fighters. Such beautiful, strong, open faces! True Ukrainians, as if they've stepped out of history books—fearless, and with a touch of mischief.

Look at our army—don't you recognize those same Cossacks writing a letter to the Turkish sultan? Their banter is full of curses, jokes, and defiance; this is an army of free people fighting by their own will! A Zaporozhzhian force that chooses its own leaders and carries itself with dignity—not some cannon fodder for commanders, but fierce, determined individuals, real Cossack warriors!

And it's not just the army—look at our civilians, laughing in the face of death, stopping enemy tanks with their bare hands! Have you seen the video of those men walking down a village road, shouting and chasing off Russian military vehicles? Unarmed! In baggy clothes, exhausted and worn, but they march together, and the enemy retreats before them.

These are the same people who have been disillusioned with their government, stuck with meager wages and pensions, with few prospects and no fancy degrees. But look at how they've risen when an invader set foot on their land!

These are the quarrelsome Kaidashes who, in a moment of truth, managed to reconcile and are now united, fighting the devil together. These are the Paraskas and Palazhkas who march up to armed Russian soldiers, unstoppable, curses pouring from their mouths. They're not just fearless—they're terrifying!

We are experiencing a moment of clarity, seeing our country and our people as if under X-ray. We see our true essence—the very thing that makes us Ukrainian. Even those who never considered themselves particularly patriotic feel it now. This ancient force is simply emerging through us today. Because this is a moment of absolute unity, where the great and the small stand together against the onslaught of a new Batu Khan.

There was no such unity during the Maidans—back then, we were divided politically, and some remained indifferent, watching from the sidelines. Today, there are no indifferent people. Even those who habitually spat at their feet and waved dismissively, saying nothing would ever change, have risen up.

The enemy has stepped onto our land and awakened not just the people but the force that makes us who we are. The force of our land and all the generations of ancestors who rest within it.

This is the moment of truth.

The stranger

On the evening of Wednesday, February 23, 2022, I went to the cinema in Kyiv with friends to see a new film by a Ukrainian director. We had a nice dinner and drank a bottle of good wine, after which we went to bed. We went to sleep as successful people, members of the middle class, with our lives planned out months in advance, citizens of a normal European country. On Thursday morning, I was supposed to wake up, put on a white shirt, board a plane, and fly to Vilnius to present the translation of my book at a literary fair. In short, it was an ordinary, normal life, just like the lives of hundreds of millions of other Europeans.

But on Thursday morning, we woke up in hell. Kyiv was being bombed in the dark, and the dogs were either howling in fear or barking wildly, their eyes fixed on the sky. For a moment, it seemed like it was just a nightmare. The sounds of explosions from a distance were like something otherworldly—like when you dive underwater in the bathtub and your heartbeat thunders in your ears. It felt as if something was exploding deep inside of us. I'll be honest with you: it was terrifying.

It's been six days since then, during which explosions and deaths have become our daily routine. From peaceful, ordinary people who used gadgets and liked funny memes on the internet, we turned into human beings with a single goal: to survive, to protect our loved ones, to preserve our home and our country. A week ago, I was the only one in my circle who believed in the onset of a Russian invasion, but even I couldn't imagine the bombing of cities and street battles in the capital

of my country. Call me naïve, but I thought that after World War II, such a war in Europe was impossible, that we had all learned at least some lessons. I was wrong.

Because this is not just a war; it's far worse—today, in Ukraine, there is the ongoing mass destruction of the Ukrainian people. This is not a war where two armies meet on the battlefield; it's an atrocity, where Russian troops attack peaceful Ukrainian cities in the most cowardly way. Russian soldiers don Ukrainian military uniforms, seize Ukrainian combat vehicles, fire trucks, and ambulances before launching terrorist attacks. Russian saboteurs in civilian clothing infiltrate peaceful Ukrainian cities and unleash terror, resorting to the murder of civilians and trying to sow panic. Is this war? This is terrorism, against which even the Taliban seems a model of morality and military honor.

The Russians appear in our cities in white doctor's coats, in the uniforms of our firefighters and rescuers, attaching Ukrainian flags to their clothes and equipment, planting explosives in residential neighborhoods, and taking civilians hostage. This is not a war between two armies; it's like another film from the *Alien* series, where an unknown form of life not only creeps at you from every crack but also disguises itself as one of your own. It's not just criminal; it's shameful, cowardly, and vile. I always thought that military officers could not stoop to such baseness, but it turns out that in the Russian army, the concept of military honor has atrophied. Just like in the Russian people, who still remain silent and do not protest against this disgusting war.

Amid this horror, there is another reality—the reality of Ukrainians who are striving to maintain their human dignity and help others. Hundreds of thousands are fleeing from shelling, while millions in relatively calmer cities are coming together to greet, feed, warm, and provide shelter to those in need. People are opening their homes to strangers they've never met; from morning to night, volunteers are organizing, transforming school gyms to accommodate refugees, purchasing medicines for cities on the front lines, and weaving camouflage nets for Ukrainian soldiers.

During this terrifying time, caregivers and psychologists distract refugee children with games, while local residents bring them toys. These remarkable people conceal their tears; after delivering humanitarian aid, they quickly return to their cars, where their emotions are allowed to spill over. We withhold our tears because we must stay resilient and lift one another up. But inside, everyone longs to cry—tears of both tenderness and fury. We grieve for the life we once knew, which, only six days ago, felt normal, but will never return.

At this very moment, while the Russians are shelling dozens of small and large Ukrainian cities, the president of my country is appealing to the EU about Ukrainian membership. I didn't vote for Zelensky, and it's important for me to emphasize this because what we are fighting for is not only the fight for Ukraine but also for Europe. We are fighting for democracy, for an individual's right to choose, a nation's right to self-determination, and for human rights and dignity. We have different political views, speak different languages, pray or consider ourselves agnostics, read different books, and listen to different music, but today we are united and ready to die for this right to diversity. For this diversity is the foundation of Europe, the bedrock of respect for all—such different, yet equally beautiful—people. Russia wants to destroy this diversity, it seeks to destroy Ukraine simply because we are not like them, because we have our own opinion about our future.

That's why I strongly support President Zelensky and appeal to all people of good will in Europe: recognize our right to become EU members in the future, send us a signal of support. After the war, we will negotiate the terms and procedures, but right now, we need only one thing: for your beacon to shine and guide us in this terrible darkness. Because hope is our greatest shortage today, and it is hope that gives strength and courage. Give us this hope, show us that we are not alone.

I wrote this text over the course of an hour—and it was a beautiful hour because I didn't read the news about bombings and deaths. This is what I can do today—write. Because I'm a writer, that's my job, although it feels shameful to talk about it under these circumstances. They are trying to push us back into the prehistoric, cave-like times when literature and writing weren't needed. This is a battle between the modern world and the dark past, the war of 2022, waged by strangers who, for no reason, decided to destroy our lives.

The war has been going on for six days. For six days, I've lived with the feeling that we've all plunged underwater, hearing our heartbeat, though in reality, it's the explosions thundering in our once peaceful cities. Help us rise from this dreadful water. Don't let us drown.

—March 1, 2022

Evacuation

I will tell you about how I left Kyiv on the evening of February 24, 2022. There were at least a million similar experiences that day, but I will still write down my own, not at all unique memory, so that later this fragment can become part of the larger mosaic of that terrible day—something akin to a biblical exodus.

On February 24, I woke up in Kyiv at dawn to the sound of explosions. That morning, I was supposed to fly from Zhuliany to Vilnius for the presentation of the Lithuanian translation of my book, but, of course, I didn't go anywhere. When the first missiles struck, life in the capital changed forever.

I spent the night at a friend's house. It was six in the morning, and Katya, my friend Pavlo's wife, immediately started packing to leave with their son and friends to relatives in Khmelnytskyi. Pavlo took hunting rifles out of the safe and said he was going to fight. But Katya asked him to fill up the car first for the journey. Pavlo agreed and disappeared for two hours. As it turned out, he had gone almost to the other end of Kyiv because there was a gas station there where he had a fifty kopeck discount per liter of fuel. The full-scale war had begun, and Pavlo was thinking about discounts—that's how, in that moment, the existential shock of a person facing the horrors of the future manifested itself.

Katya and the child left, Pavlo got ready and headed to the military enlistment office in his district. I stayed at his house on the outskirts of Kyiv, in the direction of Zhytomyr, stuck in limbo. I needed to somehow get to Chernivtsi to pick up my family, who were visiting my mother-in-law, and take them home to Uzhhorod. But I didn't have my own transport; I had come to Kyiv by train. The news and social media were broadcasting the traffic collapse live at the capital's exits: millions of people were fleeing west.

There was another absurd detail—my suitcase. As I was preparing for a tour packed with presentations and interviews, my suitcase was mostly filled with white shirts and jackets. It's a strange wardrobe choice, to say the least, for someone possibly heading to the army or escaping an encircled city across the fields. The only valuable item in that suitcase was a block of yellow Camel cigarettes, which I was bringing for my Lithuanian friend—for some reason, he believes that Ukrainian cigarettes have better, more natural tobacco. In my university days, I read numerous memoirs by Ukrainian political prisoners, and they all emphasized that in extreme circumstances, cigarettes turn into a form of valuable currency.

Later on, I teased Pavlo many times about his trip for the discount, but that morning, I was also in a state of wild numbness and fear. Do you know what I did during the first twelve hours of the full-scale invasion? I was texting with foreign acquaintances. I simply sat by the TV, switched channels, read the news, and responded to hundreds of messages I was receiving from friends and colleagues all over the world. They were worried, hastily expressing their concern, assuring me of their support, inviting me to stay with them, asking for updates. I sat there, systematically responding to these messages for hours, as if paralyzed or hypnotized.

My evacuation was arranged by my wife. Before that, she had called me several times, asking about my plans. I told her that for now, I needed to wait a bit until the situation became clearer. Later, she called me again and told me that she had found a car that was leaving Kyiv for Chernivtsi in the evening—my publisher's brother, Ivan, was driving. She sent me his number, and within a few minutes, we arranged a meeting spot on the highway near Bilohorodka.

The news was reporting rapid enemy advances from the direction where I was, helicopters were flying overhead, and explosions could be heard from a distance, though it was hard to tell how far away they were. It was unsettling when I left the virtually empty neighborhood and walked to the highway. I saw a continuous line of cars going west, but they were barely moving—calling this slow crawl "progress" seemed a stretch.

At the agreed-upon location, I had to wait for the car for almost four hours, although the GPS showed Ivan that it would take twelve minutes to get there. People were fleeing Kyiv— everywhere you looked, there were lines of cars, and many people were walking along the sides of the road. It felt apocalyptic.

Looking back, it seems that I encountered Russian saboteurs that day. I realized this only a few weeks later. I was standing by the roadside, looking out for the red Audi that was supposed to pick me up. Two middle-aged men were walking down the road. They stopped near me and asked if they were heading in the right direction for Bilohorodka and if there were any *marshrutka* (shared taxi) going that way today. I told them that I had been standing there for an hour and hadn't seen any *marshrutka*. They didn't understand the word "hour"—*hodyna* in Ukrainian—and asked something about a poisonous snake—*gadyna* in Russian—instead. Then they continued walking. A few weeks later, I recalled something I hadn't had time to process in the moment: both of them had identical yellow-and-blue ribbons on their jackets. First, it was strange that two different people had the same ribbons; second, at that time, no one wore such ribbons on their clothes. Ukrainians wear them during revolutions to visually declare their position, but before the invasion, there was no need to manifest patriotism, as everyone supported Ukraine. This mystery remains unsolved.

Ivan arrived as dusk was settling. His car turned out to be a red convertible! Yes, this is something worth remembering for the rest of my life: on the first day of the full-scale invasion, I left Kyiv in a white dress shirt, riding in a red Audi convertible!

In the four-seat car, there were five of us, plus each person had a suitcase or backpack on their lap. Three guys and two girls—my companions were all from Bukovyna. The driver, Ivan, ran a construction business in Kyiv, Pavlo was a student, Roksolana, Ivan's girlfriend, was preparing children for exams, and Olya offered manicure services. We all agreed to visit Olya for a manicure after the war, but at that moment, it felt like it would be just a few weeks, a month at most.

It was a terrifying, exhausting, and endless journey. A giant anthill was trying to crawl out of the capital, but it was getting in its own way, creating obstacles, choking on the number of cars. There were no traffic controllers or police officers on the roads. All the vehicles were packed with people and belongings—that evening, Kyiv reminded me of popular images from India. The short February day ended with a cold, dark drizzle. Aircraft were flying overhead constantly—it was unclear whether they were ours or the enemy's. Military vehicles appeared rarely on the streets. At the sight of another armored personnel carrier, the column of vehicles would start honking encouragingly, as if to say "thank you."

We spent almost ten hours just getting out of the city. When we finally made it onto the wide Zhytomyr highway, we were faced with a terrifying sight: all six lanes of the highway were clogged with cars heading one way. The vehicles were even driving in the opposite lanes, blocking any chance for individual vehicles heading toward the capital to pass. Seeing the endless string of red lights in the dark, stretching across all the lanes of the country's main artery, I felt a dull pain. For a moment, a sense of cowardice rose up, and it seemed like this was what it looked like—defeat, flight, shame. Those were the seconds, minutes, and hours when we didn't know if our country would even exist tomorrow, or if we would be alive at dawn the next day.

However, despite the chaotic exodus, there was a certain polite order within this column of cars. There was no aggression or meanness, as often happens during times of panic and attempts to escape. A similar atmosphere prevailed during the revolution on Maidan: there were countless people, all under the shadow of mortal danger, yet everyone supported one another. If someone left the column to pull over, use the restroom, or fix their car, they were let back into the flow without issue. At gas stations, there were lines that stretched for over half a mile, but people refrained from cutting ahead; they maintained order. Mothers with children were allowed to move ahead to the restrooms and shelves with food.

I witnessed a situation where an elderly man in line for fuel asked for gas without money—and seven people offered to pay for him. By the pumps stood heroic gas station workers who did not abandon their posts, flee, or rush home to their families. They stoically carried on, fully aware of how crucial their work was at that moment. It was deeply moving to see all of this, to be a part of this collective effort, and, in a moment of epochal trial, to feel pride in our people.

With every few hundred kilometers from the capital, the road became clearer, and our speed increased. We all feverishly read the news on our phones, exchanging messages from friends and acquaintances. As often happens in such situations, that night it felt as though we—the passengers in the car—had bonded forever and would now meet often after the war, become friends, christen each other's children, and host parties together. It was an illusion: after that, we never saw each other again and didn't even create a group chat. It turned out that the war would forge situational alliances of dozens of people every day, and living through this camaraderie would be intense and passionate but would resemble a meteorite, burning brightly but briefly.

We were fortunate because, after Zhytomyr, we turned south toward Khmelnytskyi and Chernivtsi, while the main part of the column continued westward toward Lviv. There was only one truly terrifying moment: in the morning, we passed through Starokostiantyniv, home to a military airfield, and the sky there was teeming with dozens of military planes and helicopters. They flew low, almost skimming the highway and rooftops, and there were so many that it seemed the sky was filled with a flock of black metal crows. It turned out the equipment had been scrambled under a combat alert: missiles were once again heading toward Ukraine, and the command was trying to save the aircraft.

After a day and a half, we arrived in Chernivtsi. The journey, which in peacetime would have taken four times less, left us exhausted and embittered. The second day of full-scale war was underway; we were tired, sleep-deprived, and hungry—and that only heightened the anxiety.

We parted ways as if it were for the last time, uncertain whether we would survive or meet again. The road ahead held countless challenges and trials, but we had taken that first journey of the war together.

Kill lists

On the third night after the start of the full-scale invasion, I slept with an axe under my pillow.

This was preceded by a rather strange situation, which today seems almost comical but at the time felt deeply unsettling. I'll try to recount everything from the beginning.

When the full-scale war broke out, I was in Kyiv, but the next day, I set off for Chernivtsi, where my wife and our daughter were staying with my mother-in-law. On the morning of February 26, my phone rang, and an unfamiliar number appeared on the screen. I answered the call and heard a woman's voice with a strong Caucasian accent. Speaking in broken Russian, the woman asked if I was already home in Chernivtsi and tried to gather information about my location.

It was very strange and even felt threatening to me—especially when, after I asked a counter-question, the woman abruptly ended the call, and the number immediately went out of service (and, incidentally, left no digital traces in any messaging apps).

In the atmosphere of widespread paranoia, this situation greatly alarmed my wife and me. I should remind you that just a few days before the invasion—on February 21, 2022—American officials announced that Russia had prepared so-called kill lists of Ukrainians who were to be targeted for elimination first. These lists supposedly included government representatives, ATO veterans, leaders of patriotic movements across various oblasts, and prominent cultural figures.

I do not belong to any of these groups, but I do have one peculiar episode in my biography. In 2017, I received an invitation from an unknown Russian journalist to fly to Moscow and participate as an expert on some talk show. My response was more sarcastic than sharp: I said I would be willing to come to Moscow only for Putin's funeral. This remark gained public attention at the time and was widely quoted by media outlets in both Ukraine and Russia.

Later that summer, I was invited to perform at a poetry festival in Armenia. At the time, Armenia was a pro-Russian country and part of a military alliance with Russia, so I decided to consult with Ukrainian diplomats to ensure I wasn't being invited to some hybrid propaganda event. The event itself turned out to be legitimate, but I was advised against traveling to Armenia. I was told that Armenia shares a police database with Russia, and if a criminal case had been opened against me in Russia for defamation of the authorities, I could be arrested directly at the airport in Yerevan.

Given that I have been persona non grata in Belarus since 2006 for participating in anti-government protests, I weighed all the risks and ultimately decided not to travel to Armenia on that occasion.

In the early days of the war, Russia launched a rather effective psy-op aimed at spreading panic throughout Ukrainian society. Through Telegram channels, information was disseminated—and quickly picked up by mainstream media—about alleged covert sabotage and reconnaissance groups operating across the country, marking targets and guiding Russian missile strikes. These marks—white or fluorescent paint markings—were reportedly found on infrastructure, buildings, and even asphalt throughout Ukraine.

As a result, many were convinced that Russian agents, saboteurs, and assassins were lurking around every corner. The true size of the threat was unknown at the time, so it was entirely reasonable to assume that Russian killers might target Ukrainians on kill lists anywhere in the country. This could have indeed caused even greater panic and disorientation within Ukrainian society.

This was the psychological backdrop of the evening of February 26, when I was at the home of my friend and editor, Oleksandr Boi chenko, in Chernivtsi. Together with him and another writer, Oleksandr Mykhed, we were discussing the idea of creating a volunteer initiative to help people from the cultural community in eastern Ukraine find housing with colleagues in the western regions.

That's when I received a call from my wife. With a frightened voice, she told me that about half an hour earlier, a car with tinted windows had parked outside their house on a quiet, deserted street in the suburbs of Chernivtsi. It was already dark outside, and no one had exited the vehicle—it seemed like they were either watching someone or waiting for someone.

My mind immediately pieced together the morning's caller with the Caucasian accent, the news about Russian sabotage groups, and the dark car parked outside my mother-in-law's house.

To assess the situation on the ground, Boi chenko, Mykhed, and I sprang into action. The plan was simple: our makeshift writer's combat squad would charge down the street in a car, block the road, turn on the high beams to blind the saboteurs, and I would step out with a knife to inspect the mysterious vehicle. Boi chenko would drive, I would handle the confrontation, and Mykhed, armed with some metal object, would jump out to assist me if a fight broke out.

That's pretty much how it happened—only it ended up more like a comedy. We sped into the street, I jumped out of the car, but for some reason, Boi chenko killed the engine and accidentally turned off the headlights as well. By the time he figured out how to get the lights back on, I was already talking to the driver of the supposed Russian-Chechen sabotage group.

It turned out to be a young Ukrainian guy with a girl sitting beside him. They had pulled into the empty side street because they were on a date and wanted some privacy. I checked the guy's ID, and he was registered at an address nearby.

It sounds amusing now, but that evening, the situation genuinely made our hair stand on end. That's why it's not surprising that later that night, I tucked a large axe under my pillow—at least I'd have some kind of weapon in case of a sudden attack.

However, six months after the invasion, we realized that the kill lists of Ukrainians were not a fabrication or a terrible nightmare, but a documented reality. In the fall of 2022, when the Ukrainian army liberated the occupied territories of Kharkiv, the tragic story of local Ukrainian writer Volodymyr Vakulenko came to light.

The Russian occupiers took over his native village, Kapitolivka, on March 7, just the second week of the war. Soon after, an armed group of invaders visited the Vakulenko household, taking the writer and his young son for interrogation. Volodymyr was questioned and beaten, but after a few hours, they let him return home. After this, he buried his personal diary in the garden under a cherry tree—something told him that dark times were ahead. He wanted to leave a record of the occupation, especially as a writer, and so he took care to preserve his written testimony.

(After liberation, Ukrainian writer Victoria Amelina found and unearthed the diary. In her foreword to the published version, she said it felt as if she were inside a new Executed Renaissance, the name for the more than two hundred Ukrainian artists who were arrested, imprisoned, and executed during the Stalinist purges. In the summer of 2023, Viktoria was killed during a Russian missile strike on a pizzeria in central Kramatorsk.)

On March 24, 2022, they came for Volodymyr again and took him in an unknown direction. He was never seen again. It wasn't until after liberation that a record of his burial was found in the workbook of the nearest district funeral service under entry No. 319. Later, DNA testing confirmed the authenticity of the record. Volodymyr Vakulenko had been killed with two shots from a Makarov pistol. Executed.

Was he dangerous? Volodya was a poet and an author of children's books, a person with a fiery temperament but a kind heart. He had several literary awards, but he wasn't exactly famous or influential either. He lived a punk lifestyle, far removed from the establishment and officialdom.

So, why was he killed? Because he was a Ukrainian poet. In such dark times, that was an unheard-of audacity and a colossal threat to the occupiers. The Russians indeed had orders to hunt down our cultural figures, commit genocide, kill for poetry, and execute for children's books, whose only danger to them lay in the fact that they were written in the Ukrainian language.

Over Achilles's grave

War strikes indiscriminately, but its most painful blows fall on those who were already living in hardship before it began. My acquaintance Anya couldn't leave her small town near Kyiv in time because she was taking care of her sick mother. When the shelling started and Russian troops occupied the area, both of them suffered: Anya, because she couldn't escape, and her mother, because she thought her daughter might die because of her. I don't know what their conversations entailed, but I'm sure that both were guided primarily by love. It was love that made one refuse to leave her sick mother, and the other try to persuade her daughter to flee to a safe place.

I don't know Kateryna personally, but through many friends of friends, her request to find scarce medication reached me. Her child suffers from epilepsy, so in addition to the horrors of war, the destruction of their home, and the need to flee their hometown, there was also the collapse of the logistical supply chain. Pharmacies were empty due to supply issues, and the desperate mother called all possible pharmacists, doctors, and volunteers from morning until night, asking for help.

Another family was preparing their child for a complex surgery, which became impossible to perform; the consequences of this forced delay will stay with the child for life. Another family was evacuating a brother from Kyiv, who uses a wheelchair. There was no special vehicle, so they simply carried him and placed him in a car that traveled for more than two days from Kyiv to a safe city. Two days during which a person with special needs couldn't get out of the car or even use the toilet.

At the station in Uzhhorod, I see a grandmother with her young grandchildren, all of whom arrived on an evacuation train from Kharkiv. Freezing, hungry, scared, they huddle together and move as one to avoid getting lost. Today, they will be housed in a huge sports hall, where hundreds of people sleep on mattresses. It's warm, clean, and safe there, but even in that place, these displaced people don't have a corner where they can hide from everyone and cry. Cry for their past lives, which will never return, which will never be the same as before the war.

War takes away people's right to privacy, and it is precisely this privacy that forms a person's individuality. War seeks to erase the individual stories of people and their specific names, turning them into numbers and statistics. It is symbolic that the displaced people, who receive a lot of different humanitarian aid, including clothes, often ask for the most personal and intimate items, like socks and underwear. In other words, those pieces of clothing that are not donated to secondhand shops and that people do not share with others—items that don't end up in humanitarian shipments. People fled their homes in a rush and didn't have the chance to pack the most essential things.

In the center of Uzhhorod, near one of the restaurants that has now turned into a giant free cafeteria for refugees, I see a long line of people. They mostly look down at their feet or at their phones, finding it difficult and shameful to lift their eyes. These are middle-class people who had good homes in Bucha and Irpin near Kyiv, who just a month ago flew low-cost airlines for weekend trips to European cities. Today, they are forced to wait for a portion of free hot food.

Among them are two young women, Svitlana and Mirka, who have lost almost nothing because they had nothing. Former students, they lived in Kyiv, rented an apartment together, enjoyed their carefree lives, and posted photos from nightclubs on Instagram. Like most young people, they had no savings for a rainy day. Simply because this generation of young Ukrainian Europeans never thought in terms of a rainy day, and their grandmothers, who hid money from their pensions under pillows and bought flour by the sack, seemed funny to them just a month ago.

Now, the girls stand in line for food, with no money, in a city where finding a job due to the influx of refugees is almost impossible. These girls could easily cross the border and seek refuge in some wealthy European country, but they prefer to sleep in a gym and receive their rations from charity workers because they don't want to leave Ukraine. And how could they leave when their boyfriends have taken up arms and gone to the front?

War has hundreds of thousands of faces, and all these faces are battered by grief. Today, in Ukraine, there are countless varieties of misfortune and pain, each with its own personal story and biography. However, even the people described above are the lucky ones, because they are alive. No sorrow or problem, humiliation or hardship can be compared to the fates of those who were struck by missiles in their homes or evacuation convoys.

Today, Ukraine has become the stage for ancient Greek tragedies, and by studying the biographies of the most ordinary Ukrainian people, one can explore the deep philosophical nuances of ancient literature. Because now everything here is simplified to the essence of things, to the deep and eternally recurring plots of Western civilization and the humanistic nature of humanity. To truly grasp what grief, pain, tragedy, and loss mean, visit Ukraine. And if you're searching for love, sacrifice, friendship, and goodness, you'll find them here as well.

The war in Ukraine is not a geopolitical conflict, but a battle for the very core of European civilization. It is a war for the right to dignity, the right to choose, for equality and the value of all people, for their equal right to life. For those who are healthy and those who are ill. For the rich and the poor. One can agree with the thesis that Ukraine is not an ideal state, a poor state, with lower living standards than those in Western Europe, sick with corruption and nepotism, but does such a state not have the right to exist, to choose its own political course and future?

For thousands of years, European civilization has been moving toward the establishment of the ideal of equality, respect for individuals and human communities, and support for maximum diversity. It was developing so that, in the twenty-first century, all people would be equal and have the right to their own dignity, so that the right to healthcare would be available not only to the rich but also to the poor, so that the right to vote in elections would be granted to all without exception, and so that a person in a wheelchair would have the opportunity to live with dignity and self-fulfillment.

That's why the European Union and NATO are built on the foundations of equality and respect for all: in these structures, both powerful countries like Germany and the United States and smaller, poorer countries like Slovenia or Lithuania have equal voting rights. Russia, by contrast, made the choice to deny Ukraine its independence and sovereignty, and even went further by claiming that Ukrainians, as a people, do not exist.

This is not just a war between Ukraine and Russia—it is a war for the very foundation of European identity. On February 24, the first day of Russia's invasion, a battle occurred over Snake Island, which became legendary for the iconic words spoken by a Ukrainian soldier to a Russian warship. That was when the world came to know this small rocky island in the Black Sea. Yet, amid the overwhelming flow of news, the world didn't immediately grasp that this was no ordinary island.

Snake Island is a rock located opposite the point where the Danube, the largest river in Western Europe, flows into the Black Sea. That is why it is called Snake Island: river water carried snakes into the salty sea, and they sought refuge on this piece of land. Even in ancient Greek times, this place was considered special: it was somewhere near Snake Island that Medea passed by when she was fleeing from Colchis (modern-day Georgia) and escaping enemy pursuit.

Snake Island itself was said to be raised from the seabed by the goddess Thetis to shelter the soul of her son, Achilles. Yes, the same hero of the Trojan War, whose heel became part of an ancient aphorism; according to myths and legends, it was on this island that Achilles was buried, and the Greeks built a temple over his grave. The remnants of that temple have survived to this day and were used as building material for the lighthouse on Snake Island.

One of the first battles in the war for Ukraine took place above the grave of the hero of the Trojan War, as if reminding us that Ukraine, even in Ancient Greek times, was part of the *oikoumene*, the inhabited and civilized world, standing at the origins of Europe and European identity. And today, it is this civilized European world that Ukraine is defending—at the cost of the lives of many heroes, whose courage and valor are on par with Achilles's.

The myth of the new Europe, Europe that fights and wars for its values and dignity, will henceforth be built on Ukrainian examples. Glory to the heroes!

Orientalism

There's an open secret that everyone knows, though it's rarely acknowledged, and it always comes to mind when I interact with people in the West. Even our greatest supporters and allies betray a certain condescension in their tone, signaling that they—perhaps subconsciously—believe the war happened to us because we, Ukrainians, deserved it, and they think that such a war could never happen to them because they are different, better, more Western. They say, "In Ukraine, there is a terrible war, but that's in Ukraine; it's impossible here." Because... Then you can list a hundred explanations, all of which boil down primarily to orientalism.

I fully understand their line of thought, because I myself thought the same way before February 24, 2022. It seemed to me that a Russian invasion would undoubtedly happen, but it would be limited to pinpoint military battles somewhere between Crimea and Donbas. In my worst nightmare, I couldn't have imagined missile strikes on Ivano-Frankivsk or Lviv, the destruction of Chernihiv and Trostianets, the real genocide of civilians in Kyiv oblast, or the brutal siege of Mariupol.

Similar war crimes were occurring in Syria just a few years ago, and thirty years ago, in almost neighboring Bosnia, which continues to struggle with the scars of that brutal war. I've spent many years studying the war in the former Yugoslavia, translating a dozen books on the subject, but somewhere deep down, I thought: that happened to them, but it could never happen to us. After all, having read private memoirs and books about World War II, I was convinced that Europe would never

sink into such a nightmare again. I'm certain that today, many citizens in the European Union, including those in countries neighboring us, think the same way.

Now that the war in Ukraine has been ongoing for more than a year and a half, I find myself reflecting on my thoughts about the tragic war in Syria. I lived through it emotionally, writing extensively about war crimes and the urgent need to address the suffering of refugees, while staying closely informed about the situation there. But I'll tell you the truth: I analyzed that war thinking that such a thing could never happen in Ukraine. Because we're in Europe! In Syria, there are deserts, Arabs, Muslims, fanatics, and such atrocities are possible there, but here, in our cozy Europe, something like that is unimaginable—after all, we've all learned the painful lessons of World War II! Reflecting on my attitude toward the war in Syria today, I feel shame: by that time, war had already been raging in Ukraine since 2014, even if it was only a hybrid war at that point, and I naively thought that missile strikes on cities, bombing theaters and hospitals, and the execution of civilians were not our reality. Oh, how naïve I was! How foolish and orientalist I was in my thinking.

Undoubtedly, the entire "logic" described here is typically orientalist, and what is interesting about it is the fact that it was thought by someone from the East, in this case, Eastern Europe.

Although in Syria, the Russian army also showed the world that it could often go further in crimes than even ISIS itself. It was the Russians who razed Syrian cities, used chemical weapons and prohibited munitions, and viewed the civilian population as the perfect target. And then, with truly perverted Russian cynicism, they held symphony concerts in the ruins of Aleppo, conducted by Kremlin lackey Valery Gergiev. Syria became a testing ground for the Russian army, a showroom for demonstrating their weapons, an advertising campaign aimed at creating a myth about Russian power. The West did not respond with much urgency to these war crimes, guided by the orientalist mindset that such things are expected there. This is the Middle East, such things are possible there...

As a writer and volunteer for my private (and nonrepresentative) sociocultural research, I have unique opportunities. As a volunteer, I frequently visit the eastern part of Ukraine, the Donbas and the south, where I interact with people who have survived occupation, soldiers who have seen Russians in the crosshairs of their weapons, and locals whose homes are practically situated along the front line. As a writer, I often travel to the West, touring Germany, Switzerland, giving talks in Sweden, the Czech Republic, Albania, Norway, and Poland. It is truly a very unusual experience—moving from a German library to the Ukrainian front. Many people go to Berlin, and many go to Kramatorsk, but not everyone can connect these two points.

The experience of connecting these points is often painful. It's a kind of hybrid reality, a twisted and bent space-time, where Berlin and Kramatorsk are parts of the same world but seem to exist in different galaxies. A tiny shift in space is enough to feel a huge change in time. As soon as you pass through the Ukrainian checkpoint and step onto EU territory, it feels like life here is still in the pre-February 24th phase. It's as if crossing the border in Chop, you're not only moving from one country to another, but from the 550th day of war, the 574th of February, into the 23rd.

We, Ukrainians, know that this impression is deceptive, that life has changed and will never be the same as it was before the full-scale invasion. But in the West, there is a false belief that war is not about them and not for them, that it is only possible with the wild Slavs in their backward Eastern Europe. And to soothe their conscience, they can allocate a few billion for humanitarian aid, provide—always belatedly—a bit of weaponry, and then once again immerse themselves in the illusion of their own superiority and security.

I do not condemn Western Europeans, because I too, I repeat, was like that before February 24. I believed that such a war was impossible for us, that large tank battles in the fields of Europe would never be repeated, that a scenario in which a bomb is dropped directly on a theater full of terrified people was unrealistic.

During the initial months of the war, I thought that people in the West could still be stirred into action, that we could raise our voices, and make them understand in the clearest way possible. Now I am more skeptical in my expectations: it seems that the consequences of some ideological mistakes have to be experienced firsthand—only then does the lesson sink in. Perhaps every generation must go through its own trials in order to remember that democracy, security, and peace are not free, but rather hard-won values. And each generation must win them back again, rediscover their forgotten benefits.

This war came to us not because we are Ukrainians, Orthodox, or live in Eastern Europe. The war is here because part of human nature has always been and remains pure and unmasked evil, which comes to destroy and kill. Today, evil has opened the door to Europe and is trying to strangle Ukraine in the corridor, but that doesn't mean it will stop and won't move onto the next rooms.

So, dear neighbors across the continent, don't be orientalist—protect yourselves!

Bizarre deviations

―――

Orysia returned from England in the summer of 2022.

When we met in August, she shared her doubts: on one hand, she wanted to go back because it was a chance for her son to get a British education diploma, but on the other hand, she strongly resisted returning because she was irritated by the widespread empathy and constant pity.

I had heard various complaints from Ukrainian refugees about the way they had been treated in other countries, but this was a very unique confession.

"You're acting spoiled," I tried to joke. Orysia took offense and started to explain.

She and her son were granted asylum in England in March, three weeks after the start of the full-scale invasion. Through a government program, they were hosted by a family whom Orysia described as being "100 percent English." They were an older, relatively wealthy couple living in some county that fit the textbook definition of the British countryside.

It was a one-and-a-half-story house nestled in seclusion, with walls built before World War I and a roof converted into a spacious attic in the early 2000s. A lawn so perfect it seemed straight out of jokes about England. A fireplace, a collection of paintings on the walls, a rocking chair, a dog. Comfort and old age enjoyed to the fullest: constant theater visits, shared travels, friends over for dinner on weekends, plenty of free time, and a respectable amount of money in their bank account.

"At some point, I wondered if my son and I had also become one of their retirement activities. But I immediately talked myself out of thinking that way because it's hypocritical to accuse very kind and compassionate people of treating their help as entertainment instead of simply being grateful," Orysia explained.

The English family gave her and her son the attic, so they had their own private space. They even allowed Orysia to use their car if needed. The only shared space was the kitchen on the first floor—the place where all of them inevitably crossed paths. Orysia tried her best to avoid going to the kitchen.

At first, everything was idyllic: long conversations and stories about life and family, looking through family photo albums, and shared dinners. Borsch, which Orysia cooked to introduce them to Ukrainian cuisine. Nostalgic visits to a nearby church the homeowners were eager to show off, as it was the place where they had gotten married. A picnic on the edge of the woods with a basket of fruit and long games with the dog.

After a month, a certain tension began to build in the house. Living together is hard even for close family members, let alone strangers from a completely different culture. There was a moment when the homeowner asked if everyone in Ukraine took such long showers. A week later, the hostess casually remarked that washing your hair every day isn't good for it.

The tipping point came over a bottle of wine. The hosts had a nightly ritual of sharing a bottle of wine together. They had offered Orysia a glass a few times, but after a while, they conspicuously stopped asking if she wanted one. One day, she bought a bottle of white wine at the supermarket and put it in the fridge. That evening, when she came out to pour herself a glass, the hosts gave her cold, hostile stares. The next morning, they greeted her curtly and avoided eye contact.

"You know, if I had to prove anything in court, it would be a disaster because they never said anything explicitly hurtful, nor did any of their actions seem overtly hostile. But psychological pressure was undoubtedly being exerted on me in that house. I felt it, but I couldn't explain or prove it, so at some point, I shocked myself by thinking I must be paranoid."

Orysia only understood the nature of this abuse in the summer, when she returned to Ukraine with her son for the holidays. At home, everything suddenly became clear to her.

"These wonderful people were blackmailing me. In exchange for their kindness and help, they demanded my suffering. While, in the first few weeks, I was crying all the time, they were happy because they felt like noble saviors. But when I later found the strength to live and smile, the English saw it as a betrayal of their mission."

Is it okay to drink wine when there's war in your country? Is it okay to say that you have a modern house in Ukraine, two cars in the family, a cleaning lady twice a week, summers by the sea, and skiing abroad in the winter? How do you explain to people that you're fleeing from war and missile strikes, not poverty?

These questions tormented Orysia for a long time. She felt ashamed before the English that she was wealthy and successful. She felt ashamed before her fellow Ukrainians that she was afraid for her child and had fled. She felt ashamed before her son that she sat in her attic in the evenings, too afraid to go out. She felt ashamed that, while other Ukrainians were facing immense danger and the deep grief of loss, she was tormented by some absurd, God help her, internal sense of shame.

She never returned to England.

"I'd rather be hit by a missile here, I don't want to be pitied!"

"You really are paranoid," I concluded.

"Go to hell," Orysia laughed.

***

My close friends Viktor and Violetta have ten children.

This wonderful and noisy family left for Germany immediately on February 24, 2022. They were especially worried about their son David, who has a serious genetic condition and needs daily medication that is in short supply.

It could also be phrased differently: Viktor and Violetta didn't leave—they returned to Germany. It was there that they received their higher education, got married, had their first two children, and lived in Siegen, in the western part of the country, where they started a business. But then the Orange Revolution happened, and on the wave of patriotic enthusiasm, the family returned to Ukraine to help build their homeland

After the full-scale invasion began, fate led them back to Siegen once again. Paradoxically, their older children, who, as I mentioned, were born in Germany and have spoken German since childhood, were the first to complain that they wanted to go home—to Ukraine. This came as a shock to everyone.

At first, this was dismissed as typical teenage behavior—wanting to push against the norm. Violetta, the mother of the large family, explained it this way: "They just want to get on my nerves." But the children, no longer really children since they were over eighteen, resisted all persuasion, ignored rational arguments, refused to wait out the war at German universities, and weren't drawn to the idea of building careers in the West while helping Ukraine from there. These two grown-up girls made it clear: they were returning home, and if their parents didn't support them in this, they would sever ties with them.

Later, it became clear that this wasn't an isolated incident, but the trait of an entire generation. A generation we hadn't had time to observe before the invasion, because they hadn't yet emerged from their teenage self-isolation to enter the public stage. The children of the 2000s—these were the children of a happy childhood.

My generation—sometimes referred to as the children of independence—lived through a difficult childhood in the '90s. The prevailing mood among most of my peers was understandable: a normal life was only possible by emigrating. And if one were to live in Ukraine, the starting point was to go abroad for a few years and to earn money for a car and a house.

Against this backdrop, the next generation of Ukrainians is truly striking in its mindset. They don't want to live abroad; they see other countries only as tourist destinations. Of course, this doesn't apply to all Ukrainian children, but there is a noticeable group of teenagers from middle-class families who are perfectly content with the standard of living at home. For them, even life in wealthier Western countries is filled with moments of "this is stupid," "they're so annoying," and "we're better off."

It seems we overlooked the emergence of a generation that loves Ukraine not just out of patriotism or ethnic pride, but—perhaps above all—for the quality and comfort of life. After the full-scale invasion, a new dimension of pride emerged—one rooted in the admiration for their country's resilience, standing strong like an ancient hero.

I was there when my friend Viktor brought his two eldest daughters home. They were energetically unloading things from the van and carrying them into the apartment. A neighbor, an older woman who was watching this from the side, raised her eyebrows in disbelief. She couldn't wrap her head around it. In TV shows, everyone wanted to leave, but here, the kids were returning of their own volition.

"They've lost it," she concluded.

***

Sanya drives a Lexus.

This isn't his only flaw, but it's the most noticeable one, especially abroad, especially with a Ukrainian license plate on the car.

Sanya is a farmer, and the two things he dislikes most in life are IT professionals and dentists. The reason for his dislike of dentists is obvious, but his issue with IT professionals stems from their "disconnect from the land."

"In Ukraine, everyone's obsessed with IT people as if they're the country's main potential. But I think our real strength lies in farmers. IT people don't care—they can work anywhere. They just like it here because, with their income levels, they can feel like superstars. In the West, they'd just be ordinary. On the other hand, a farmer is tied to the land, to local people. They invest in them, and they're truly willing to fight for that land," he tells me.

Sanya didn't immediately take his family to the West. In the first days of the invasion, he focused on supporting local self-defense, gave up his heavy machinery to help build defense lines, and provided free fuel to all law enforcement and volunteers in the area.

Once the situation stabilized a bit, he packed his family into the car and drove his wife and kids to Austria. They didn't ask for any help or refugee status; they simply rented an apartment in Vienna and enrolled their children in private kindergarten and school.

After making sure his loved ones were taken care of, Sanya immediately returned home. He runs a large farming operation here, employing hundreds of people, and, of course, it's spring—planting season.

There are no bigger optimists than farmers who were sowing crops in the eastern Ukrainian regions in the spring of 2022. When I spoke to him, I called it bravery, but Sanya explained it differently: not sowing would be a sin. You can't leave the land to its fate, even if you're unsure whether you'll be able to harvest the crop.

Since March 2022, Sanya has been regularly traveling back and forth between Ukraine and Austria. He visits his children and then returns to work. broad, what bothers him most are his Ukrainian license plate and bank cards. So, he hides his car in the garage and has gotten used to paying with cash.

"I should be proud of the big, successful business I've built, but instead, I feel like I'm living in some damn communist times. I've never been in government service and earned all my money honestly, but I'm ashamed to be rich. I don't want people in a Vienna restaurant to know we're from Ukraine because they'll think badly of us. I don't want them to see my Lexus because the way they treat me changes immediately. Maybe I'm overreacting, but I feel like the West is so slow to send us weapons because subconsciously they don't want us to win. Because if we do, it'll shatter the stereotype that all Ukrainians are poor and miserable. They're not ready to see us as victors," he says, his emotions boiling over.

"Oh, you poor thing, you unfortunate Euro millionaire, let me offer you my pity," I tease him.

"Just don't pity me!" Sanya laughs, forgetting that during a war, laughing is inappropriate.

Investments

Looking at all the bombed-out houses and burned neighborhoods, I thought about one thing: the most important investments should be in the intangible. In yourself, your education, experiences, emotions, and memories. They are the highest values. They are life itself.

The war has made this very clear. Because if you know a language, you have better chances of receiving support and settling abroad. If you know how to drive, you're more mobile; you can help others or at least escape quickly. If you've built social connections, developed community environments, and participated in various initiatives—you'll find it much easier to get the help you need, find the right contacts, and be more effective.

How many times have I traveled on my last bit of money, not to mention what I borrowed? But in the end, it was the right move because all those impressions, the sights, the tastes, the places I've been to, the rivers I've crossed, have stayed with me. No one can bomb or occupy that. It's my private territory.

As borders remain closed and travel feels like a distant dream, I think back and realize how fortunate I was to travel before the war. My rule was always that my visits should outnumber my age. But now, I wish I had set my sights higher and aimed for double the number of countries as my age.

Because you save up for an apartment, dream of a house, economize, upgrade your car—all of this is great, but suddenly it could all be gone. What never disappears is what you always carry with you, inside you. Memories, emotions, knowledge, skills, experiences, and relationships. These make up the most reliable deposit in life.

Flowers of victory

On September 12, 2023, I was handed an envelope from the students and teachers of a picturesque and ancient village, Korolevo, in Transcarpathia. Inside the envelope was seventeen thousand hryvnias—approximately four hundred euros—money that the children, their parents, and the teachers had raised during the celebration of the new school year.

The idea was that instead of giving flowers to the teachers, the children would drop a donation into a box to support the Armed Forces of Ukraine, whose heroism makes it possible for a Ukrainian school to exist in Korolevo and for children to continue their education even during the war. The collected funds were handed to me to purchase and prepare jeeps for the Ukrainian army.

Two weeks later, a young couple who had just gotten married came to meet me. Tetiana and Vladislav handed over thirty thousand hryvnias (approximately seven hundred euros) for a vehicle for the Armed Forces of Ukraine. The money was raised at their wedding: guests were asked not to buy flowers, but instead to donate the equivalent of the cost of a bouquet to support the Armed Forces of Ukraine.

Life goes on even during war: people are born and people die, people get married, and for the ability to marry in their own country, they wish to express their gratitude, even through a symbolic gesture like a donation to the army. This is less about the money and more about the desire to show gratitude, to demonstrate that even far from the front lines, even in the happiest moments, we do not forget those who, in the trenches, are defending our right to live.

I was reminded of this a few days ago, a thousand kilometers from my home. It happened in Krasnogruda, where, beside a tranquil lake in an old forest, lies the Miłosz Manor. Today, it houses the Borderland Foundation, but before World War II, it was where the future Nobel laureate Czesław Miłosz found respite from the bustle of the city in his relatives' estate. This very location inspired his poem "A Song on Porcelain," which now hangs at the entrance to the local Café Europa.

Nostalgically reflecting on the past shattered by the tanks of World War II, Miłosz writes about a porcelain tea set. Of all the idyllic years in Krasnogruda, he laments nothing as much—not the memories, not his youth, not the calming landscape—as the porcelain. The fragile delicacy of a porcelain cup and saucer, their exquisite beauty, becomes not only a symbol of familial comfort and peaceful times but a symbol of peace itself. When deadly, multi-ton tanks roll through the countryside, who will care about broken porcelain?

Of course, while reading Miłosz's poem, I thought about flowers. More specifically, about the symbolic act of refusing them—for the sake of supporting the Ukrainian army. During a war, if I had to choose between weapons and flowers, I would undoubtedly choose weapons. A flower is far too defenseless for these terrifying times. It serves no practical purpose, offers no tangible benefit.

Yet, a flower does have one significant function. It reminds us of beauty, of the perfection and elegance of the created world, of the fact that life holds a place not only for evil, hatred, and base instincts but also for genius, transcendence, and tenderness.

Undoubtedly, flowers are not a necessity; they cannot be used to counter tanks. Saving money on flowers is justified and needed, so I am grateful to the schoolchildren and the newlyweds for their gesture of support. But to paraphrase Miłosz: in these times, there is nothing I regret as much as the flowers left ungiven. Because one definition of war might be this: war is the time when we are forced to renounce beauty. Beauty that is impractical, fragile, ridiculous in its irrelevance, yet so essential to us all.

And so I dare to articulate another maxim: we dream of victory so that we may once again have the chance to give each other flowers.

Odesa

I confessed my love to my future wife in Odesa.

It happened on Ukraine's Independence Day, August 24, 2016, during an Okean Elzy concert at the packed Chornomorets Stadium.

The paradox is that I can recall the entire day and evening in vivid detail, but my memories of the concert itself are fragmentary. I remember us dancing to some song in the crowd, which was singing along loudly and out of sync with the lead singer, but which song was it?

I can physically recall how warm and silky the August air felt, how the breeze occasionally carried the iodized scent of the sea, and I even vividly remember my white shirt with rolled-up sleeves. I recall how, after the concert, we returned to the Odesa apartment with friends and indulged in local wine, Bulgarian bryndza, and ripe tomatoes. But I cannot remember the most important part—the words I whispered to my beloved. Because overcoming the fear of public speaking and performing in front of a large crowd is one thing, but whispering the most important words of your life into the ear of the one person who matters most is an utterly paralyzing experience.

Since that evening, Odesa has held a unique, special place in my life and personal story. It's no longer just a point on the map but a deeply cherished city, completely my own, though Odesa itself is entirely unaware of this.

I felt this incredibly acutely after the full-scale invasion of Russia began. Among thousands of pain points and countless fears, one nerve throbbed with particular intensity—Odesa. I was terrified at the thought that this city might be occupied or destroyed, that I might never be able to bring my family here and, years from now, tell my children about the love story their mother and I shared.

Perhaps this is how a country stitches itself together—on a deeply personal, emotional level. It anchors itself to a point on the map with invisible tethers and never lets go. It weaves itself into your life story, settling into the family album like a cherished photograph.

That's why one of the tasks I've set for myself after victory is to travel more actively across Ukraine: to explore its nature, meet its people, and taste its local dishes. It's our generation's great homework assignment, our duty—to rediscover our country, to fill its more than 230,000 square kilometers with faces, memories, impressions, and adventures.

And one more task, but this one is purely personal—to finally remember the song I nervously shuffled my feet to, voice trembling as I said, "I love you."

A wartime queen

There's a sad, yet somewhat ironic truth: literature lovers have it harder during wartime because their apartments and houses burn faster after missile strikes. Books ignite, paper fuels the flames—and the fire truck doesn't make it in time.

The question I hear most often from international audiences is: "What is the role of literature during war?" The answer is clear: in practice, it is negligible. In the face of widespread destruction, bullets and missiles don't choose their victims—they kill indiscriminately: readers and illiterate people alike, writers and their critics.

Of course, literature does have its influence in a broader context, as it can represent a country and its people abroad. Every war in the world sparks interest in that particular corner of the planet, and as a result, translations of books, musical productions, and museum exhibitions begin to appear in various countries. Literature delves deeper, explains, and advocates, making it an ideal tool for cultural diplomacy during times of upheaval.

There are even stories about how a book saved a soldier's life. I've seen such accounts on social media myself: here's a photo of a man holding a book with a bullet lodged inside. This is a story that has become something of a wandering legend: I've heard it told about a philosophical book by Seneca, a novel by Ernst Jünger, and, of course, the Bible. Similar examples are known from many wars, so this is either the reproduction of a familiar tale adapted to a local context, or perhaps sometimes a book in a pocket does indeed save its reader from a sniper's bullet.

But a bulletproof vest is far more reliable than a book. And having a weapon in your hand makes it possible to fight back against the aggressor and drive out the bloodthirsty invaders. That's why, during my talks abroad, I constantly ask my audience: tell your governments that we need more weapons! Between a ton of Plato's books and a ton of bulletproof vests, I, as a writer, would choose the vests. These are the laws of wartime.

War is not a time for literature. During war, it is difficult, if not impossible, to write. It's hard to concentrate, to maintain a logical train of thought; under the onslaught of news and stress, intellectual life becomes fragmented and chaotic, while an emotional pendulum swings a person between extremes. In such circumstances, it's nearly impossible to write a novel that requires years of focused effort. It's hard enough even to read one attentively!

However, there is one form of literature that suddenly gains strength during wartime and reclaims its long-lost position from antiquity. This is poetry—the queen of wartime. Forgotten and neglected by almost everyone, relegated to the highest shelf of elitism, niche appeal, and irrelevance in the modern world, poetry rises to prominence from the onset of war.

Many friends of mine who were forced to become refugees, even temporarily, have told me that they included a book in their bug-out bag. That book symbolized comfort, the intimacy of a home library, home itself. Most often, that book was a collection of poetry. Why? At first glance, poetry seems impractical and irrelevant. But that's precisely what makes it so symbolic: if you're going to take something with you, let it be something exquisite and defiantly impractical—a testament that it is not a frightened animal fleeing bombs and fires, but a human being.

Thanks to its brevity, poetry is well-suited for reading even in bomb shelters. Under the light of a flashlight, you can read a poem in two minutes and savor it for much longer. You close the book for the time being, but the poem stays with you. A collection of poetry becomes an endless adventure—you can learn it by heart, open it at random, or rhythmically repeat it to yourself under your breath.

I remember how I returned to reading in the second week of the war. It was Taras Shevchenko's birthday, so I decided to find a lesser-known quote of his and post it on social media. I took *Kobzar* from the shelf and began flipping through it. I read one poem, then another, and kept going. By the third hour, I caught myself thinking that I was hooked, that I couldn't tear myself away—these poems written two hundred years ago were about me, about us, about our time. Goosebumps rose on my skin—this is how these lines worked. Their brilliance didn't need to be proven—they worked on a physical level.

Since then, I've been revisiting poetry more actively—Shevchenko, Stus, and other Ukrainian poets persecuted and killed by Russia, as well as old favorites like Ovid, Cavafy, Ginsberg, Verlaine, Miłosz, and Zadura, who had long been forgotten. Audio versions of Homer's *Odyssey* and *Iliad* for listening during long drives. It's an absolute mishmash—chaotic and inconsistent—but that's the beauty of poetry: you can read a poem, take a pause, switch to something else, choose based on your mood, or simply grab a book off the shelf at random.

But the most important thing is this: poetry isn't just something to read, it's something to write! A poem is written in the mind, in the heart; it doesn't require special conditions, technique, or a studio. Over the past year and a half of war, poetry has returned to its original purpose—to help people share their pain, hope, and thoughts. Among all forms of art, poetry has become the mass tool for emotional self-care.

Often these poems are imperfect, awkward, cacophonous, banal. But they serve the primary function of art—expressing a person's inner state, emotions, and hopes. These poems aren't meant for literary history; snobs and critics might label them amateurish, but they offer relief, others see themselves in them, and through that connection, the magic of words takes effect. (By the way, something similar has happened with painting: today, the greatest emotional power comes from children's drawings, which I often deliver from children to their fathers who are on the front lines; it's impossible to imagine a better picture than one drawn by a clumsy child's hand. When you look at such a "primitive" drawing, you can't help but think it's God who guides their hand!)

Recently, I saw a story on the Instagram of a friend of mine, where she shared a screenshot of a conversation with her husband, who is now at war. He had gone on duty and, unable to sleep that night, wrote her a poem about love and the morning. When she woke up, the first thing she saw in her messenger was this poem. After reading it, she cried. The poem is almost comical in its simplicity, from a literary standpoint it's truly awful, but from a human perspective, it's actually so beautiful!

I believe that the great novels about this war will be written only after it's over, as good prose requires time, distance, and emotional detachment. In contrast, poetry needs the opposite: timeliness, closeness, and emotional engagement. Poetry requires feeling, burning passion, and it needs to be done now, in this very moment. For this reason, poetry, by its nature and power, has become the queen of wartime, the ruler of all arts.

The main thing is to survive until September

In early June, I received an order for an autographed set of my books. The order form specified that the books should be signed for Tolik and sent to Novomykolaivka. When I got to the post office, I learned that there are at least twenty-five Novomykolaivkas in Ukraine, scattered across different regions, so I had to message Tolik to clarify which one he meant.

He replied that it was the Novomykolaivka in Zaporizhzhia region. I looked it up on the map: the settlement is located between Zaporizhzhia and the front line, very close to the occupied territories. We started a conversation: I asked how things were going, how life was there, and if I could help with anything. Tolik replied that he wasn't local, but a Ukrainian soldier fighting in the southern direction, and Novomykolaivka was simply the closest settlement with postal services.

It was the beginning of summer, and all conversations were focused on the Ukrainian counteroffensive in the south, so naturally, I asked him more questions. He told me that in his prewar life he had been a photographer. He was mobilized in the fall of 2022; he didn't want to join the army as a volunteer, but also didn't evade the draft. In the spring of 2023, he underwent training in Germany, where he learned to operate Western armored vehicles, coordinated tactics, and NATO combat strategies. He came back with a strong impression that theorists were teaching practitioners. At least the food was good there, he added.

By June, he had already been promoted to sergeant and was commanding a combat vehicle. He said the offensive had actually started, but their brigade was not yet involved; they were waiting for their turn. He shared cautious optimism, saying that there were plenty of them, a lot of new and effective equipment, and the enemy's outdated army wouldn't be able to stop them, although the losses would be severe. There was enough of everything, and everything was working well. The weakest link in the newly formed Ukrainian units was the number of unmotivated soldiers who didn't want to fight and were afraid of fighting. But still, by spring, they would be on the Azov Sea.

After discussing both civilian and military matters, I asked about the reason for our contact: who was he ordering my books for? Tolik replied that they were for himself. In his youth, he had loved my poetry and would give poetic books to his girlfriend. Once, they came across a video online where I was reading the poem "You'll Wake Up in the Morning and Say," and after that, they both got hooked. They memorized the poem, and together they came to my performances in Lviv. Tolik had even tried to write poems back then, but only for himself. Later, he gave it up, broke up with that girl, but still sometimes enjoys reading books to set his mood. When he saw a review of my book on Facebook, he decided to order it for himself, to take his mind off the military and the war.

I signed the books, added a few small gifts to the package, and sent it to Novomykolaivka. A few days later, I received a message from him on Messenger: "Thank you, I got them!" I checked in again to see how things were going and asked him to take care of himself. Tolik replied, "We're doing our job," and then added, "The main thing is to make it to September. Just like in your poem."

I do indeed have a poem called "The main thing is to make it to September." I wrote it when I was a bright-eyed student, who, during the summer break, had said goodbye to his girlfriend and dreamed of waiting until autumn to see her again at the university. That's why I wrote: "The main thing is to survive until September!" Back then, fifteen years ago, I had no idea that one day a soldier from the front lines would quote this poem. This says a lot about our army: the counteroffensive is driven by soldiers who quote poetry.

Well, I guess it was worth writing them—at least because, decades later, they became a kind of tool for mutual understanding. To write, so that words, sentences, literature become a chain that connects people and creates micro-communities. So that later, thanks to literary recognition, we can raise tens of millions of hryvnias and buy hundreds of jeeps, which help the armed forces every day, bring victory closer, and save specific lives. It turns out that poems, books, literature can do that too.

I write to Tolik once every few weeks, so as not to bother or interfere. But every day, I check our chat page and see when he was last online. I'm writing these words in August, and the messenger shows that he logged in today—so, he's alive. Hang in there, my friend! The main thing is to survive until September! Until September, after the victory.

The cultural front

Few things annoy me more than the phrase "cultural front," as it diminishes the significance of both the front and culture.

There is only one front. People are killed, injured, maimed, and even if they come out of it alive, the psychological impact of it all will haunt them for the rest of their lives. To compare the front with sitting on a stage in a European capital, which eventually leads to a dinner at an expensive restaurant surrounded by refined people, is blasphemy.

But this doesn't mean that culture is unimportant or irrelevant. In many ways, it is culture that helps us form an international coalition in support of Ukraine and secure Western weapons. Because thanks to culture, the world learns about Ukrainians, sees us as equals, and understands that Russian statements about the non-existence of the Ukrainian people are Nazi bullshit.

While in the East our independence is fought for in the trenches, in the West it is fought in opera boxes and university lecture halls. Seeing the richness and modernity of Ukrainian culture, and understanding the complexity and depth of its history, the Western audience (who, as voters, influence their government's policies) begins to grasp the magnitude of Russia's crimes against Ukrainians, recognizing the outlines of a real and centuries-long genocidal intent to this war. The result is empathy and a sense of solidarity, which is converted into support through weapons. So, culture has an impact—there's no doubt about that.

We should not underestimate the influence of culture within the country. It is culture that strengthens society, builds invisible bridges between regions and people, and forms not just an imagined but a very real community that defines itself. It establishes boundaries with outsiders, creating a mental (or cultural?) divide that ultimately becomes a state border on the map.

The Russians are not destroying Ukrainian museums and theaters with missiles by chance; they are looting exhibitions and collections, burning books from school libraries, and in a fit of frenzied contempt, shooting at Ukrainian monuments, as they did with the monument to Taras Shevchenko in Borodianka. By destroying Ukrainian culture—at least the tangible aspects they can reach with their hands and bullets—they are undermining the very foundations of the Ukrainian people's existence, eroding its distinctiveness, and attempting to erase boundaries in order to further absorb Ukrainians into the syphilitic body of the Russian Empire.

Culture is incredibly important and not just during wartime. But the phrase "cultural front" offends and diminishes culture, as it denies its primary function. The "cultural front" is an oxymoron, because culture is the antithesis of war.

War is destruction—a fiery chaos that ravages people, animals, plants, the soil, and the planet itself. It tears apart the intangible—social bonds, belief in humanity, and the very foundations of decency. Therefore, the opposite of war is not merely peace. Peace is an interim state between war and its true opposite. For if the essence of war is destruction, then the antonym of war is creation—culture. Considering the history of our civilization and the Ukrainian context, culture is best compared to a field: sowing and cultivating, a settled way of life that counters nomadic barbarism, and work with a long-term vision—waiting for the harvest.

During the scorching first summer of the war, Russian forces relentlessly shelled the fields in the south of Ukraine. Wheat and other crops, sown before the full-scale invasion, were set ablaze. I vividly remember the acrid smoke rising in the vast steppe sky. It was a clear threat: we will deny you food, and in doing so, deny you life. Yes, war is about destruction, while life is about creation and cultivation—after all, in agriculture, we speak of cultivating varieties. Everything comes from culture.

Degradation

If I had to choose just one word to describe myself after a year of war, I would bitterly say: degradation.

Yes, of course, the war has strengthened me in some ways and taught me things, helped me test my friends and acquaintances, added new skills and contacts, convinced me that I can quickly change my field of work and succeed there. As therapists would say, the war took me out of my comfort zone and put me to a resilience test. It brought me together with wonderful new people who were not part of my previous environment, softened my snobbish arrogance, and expanded my horizons. It knocked down some of my pretensions, but in some ways, it also added to them.

Yes, I've gathered a lot of material for new texts and books, acquired new knowledge, and I hope I've managed to transform it into a more mature form of wisdom. For a writer, great catastrophes are always a source of creativity because upheavals reveal human nature, helping us understand the world and the laws of life. And this then expresses itself in characters and plots, themes, and ideas.

Yes, I've witnessed what human solidarity really means. How the best in people emerges, how an ordinary, average person—in sociological terms—becomes a hero, a savior, how ancient allusions appear in their life. Perhaps this is the most monumental thing one can see in a human life. This is what it means to live in an era of great trials, in the years that future generations will memorize in history lessons. But I would give everything to have avoided this fate, to be able to move from the screen to the audience in this cinematic session.

Because when I am alone with myself, I must admit: during the war, I have degraded terribly. It's painful to look at myself in the mirror. The heavy psychological detachment: Is this really me, is this my life? I long to wake up from this nightmare and return to the normalcy that existed before February 24, 2022. We criticized it back then and thought it imperfect, but now, with time, it seems ideal. Unfortunately, it will never be the same again. Something new will come, perhaps even better in the distant future, but that past life with its beautiful routine will never return.

War devours time, people, buildings, and territories. It's like shifting sand, swallowing everything around us. War drags us back to a more primitive level of existence. It's a descent that quickens with every passing month—until we find ourselves at the Neanderthal stage, drinking from rivers and cooking over an open fire in the wilderness. War strips away our civilizational veneer, diminishes us, erases cultural layers, and reduces us to our raw physical form.

The war has already stolen a year and a half of my life, irreversibly consumed it, without even a sign of protest. And since there seems to be no end in sight, it's unclear how much more it will take. A year and a half of the most productive, best years when I could create, write, travel, enjoy time with my family, have fallen into the abyss and there wasn't even a splash. War has no bottom.

My God, how many books I haven't read in the past year and a half! Never mind the ones I haven't written, but think of all the valuable books I've missed! How intellectually degraded I've become, falling behind the trends that dominate the world because I lack the time to read, follow, and be interested.

How degraded my language has become! I communicate with some stripped-down version of my previous language—

coarser, poorer, more primitive. Swearing has replaced filler words and polite expressions, synonymic rows have withered, complex subordinate and coordinate constructions have broken down into meager fragments of sentences. Now I understand where Hemingway's signature telegraphic style came from...

How degraded my emotions have become! The intensity of events and impressions is so high that everything has burned out. Tears no longer well up when I see photographs of yet another residential building destroyed by a Russian rocket. I've turned to stone, become stiff—where has that tender poet gone, the one who once felt every emotional surge so deeply? I've passed so many ruined villages and towns that I no longer take photos of the ruins. When I see a whole building or a large object, I automatically project onto it a scheme of possible destruction. The strangest thing is that I don't even hate the Russians anymore, as I did at the beginning of the war: I have no emotional energy left for that. Now, toward that despicable people and their country, which is the embassy of Lucifer on planet Earth, I feel only indifferent apathy. It's as if my dreams have come true, and they simply don't exist anymore.

My body has degraded too, it's tired, worn out. Bags under my eyes, gray hair, sporadic failures in the digestive or cardiovascular systems—all the consequences of constant stress, locked inside animal fear, working beyond my physical limits. My old friends, whom I meet and see every day, have aged so much in these years, such sorrow in their eyes! A generation branded by war, forever bound to carry this collective trauma with 40 million specific faces.

Even my dreams have degraded. Or rather, they've grounded themselves. I only want one thing—victory and the end of the war, a return to what was our past life with its little daily worries and plans. Former ambitions seem empty and meaningless when the only desire and the only plan is to survive.

Well, over these one and a half years, I've become a worse and older version of myself, simpler, hardened, bristling. Despite everything, the outcome is a plus: I'm alive.

War is not only about heroes

Thirty-four-year-old Oleksandr had not left his home for almost fourteen months. He and his wife Solomiya set out from Kyiv on February 28, 2022. I met them in Uzhhorod on March 10. They stayed with friends for a few days along the way, but their later attempts to find a place to live proved futile as everything was already occupied, rented, or fully packed.

The couple had planned to locate a place closer to Ukraine's western border, ensuring that, "in case of an emergency," they could flee more easily. However, crossing the border right away would prove impossible because the state prohibited men of military age from doing so, and Oleksandr lacked any grounds to seek a deferment from military service.

Friends of friends asked me to help Oleksandr and Solomiya find a place to live. It was then I heard, quite by accident, that my friend from Uzhhorod had decided to rent his tiny Khrushchev-era apartment to internally displaced persons (IDPs). His mother used to live there, and he never got around to renovating or selling it after she passed away. At the beginning of the full-scale invasion, such real estate in Uzhhorod, which is on the border with the EU, suddenly became a luxury. Only the floors of school gyms were free of charge, whereas this was a separate apartment with a decent owner wanting prewar era rent. What a bargain!

Oleksandr is a prime example of Kyiv's successful middle class. He has a good salary, owns a mortgaged two-floor apartment, and an electric car. He has visited several countries, has insurance covering all expenses, and is building his retirement fund. He is an IT specialist and department head at one of the state corporations. He's the kind of person whose achievements in life would serve as an example to others.

The war broke something in him. He was driven from Kyiv by blind fear, but in Uzhhorod, which has not been under threat of missile strikes, it did not disappear. Fear took root inside him, initially manifesting as long-healed gastritis that persistently nagged, troubled, and eroded his body. Eventually, it metastasized into his soul, completely subduing and paralyzing the man. Oleksandr stopped venturing outside his home. Rather than fearing Russian missiles, his concern shifted to military patrols distributing mobilization summonses.

One way or another, it was the fear of death—first from enemy bombs and then from death on the front line. While it is entirely natural to feel fear, the intensity of Oleksandr's fear surpassed the usual bounds of natural and normal emotions, evolving into a form of paranoia—a sort of persecutory obsession.

During short walks or trips to the supermarket in the evenings, Oleksandr felt as if someone was about to tap him on the shoulder from behind. And then the military summons would come, followed by being forcibly escorted to the military registration and enlistment office, deployment to the front line, and, inevitably, death. His imagination was fueled by the terrifying tales he encountered on social media—stories of the military sealing off mall exits to distribute mobilization notices to every man inside, of patrols visiting stadiums and beaches. Eventually, he reached the conclusion that it was safer to remain home. Fortunately, there was plenty of work to keep him occupied. After the liberation of the Kyiv oblast and the passing of May 9, Russia's self-imposed deadline for complete victory, which everyone was so afraid of, people returned to their homes en masse. The state corporation where Oleksandr worked decided to resume full operations and called on all staff, especially top management, to return to the office. After weighing all the pros and cons, he wrote a letter of resignation, deciding that he could get enough IT work to freelance at home without missiles regularly falling on Kyiv and patrols lurking on the streets with summonses. Uzhhorod seemed safer, and in the end, it was.

Solomiya, Oleksandr's wife, supported her husband's decision in every way—so much so that my friends thought it was actually her decision. She was worried about her husband and did not want him to go to the front. It wasn't that he was unfit; quite the contrary, Oleksandr was a healthy man. But in her opinion, he could contribute more effectively from the homestead front. At the very least, he could generate income online from abroad, working remotely and paying taxes to Ukraine, thereby supporting the economic front, so to speak. And, after all, how could he possibly, being faint of heart, a nerd, and a pacifist, engage in combat? Even Solomiya had more of a belligerent streak.

I found out about all this as a *fait accompli*, given that we had not had a chance to see each other since our first meeting in March. I first heard about Oleksandr's phobia on New Year's Eve. My friends wanted to prank him, knocking on the door and pretending to be mobilization officers. This joke did not seem very amusing to me, especially since by the winter of 2022, I had already heard of many instances where men had not ventured outside of their homes for months. The fear of mobilization became widespread, with daily obituaries from Bakhmut casting a dark shadow over everything, and there were no lines of volunteers outside of military enlistment offices anymore. This is the sad and unvarnished truth.

In May 2023, the couple decided to separate, and Solomiya filed for divorce. That was the moment when I heard the whole story from my acquaintance who had rented them the apartment. Long story short, the couple could not stand being locked in an uncomfortable space for such a long time. They managed to survive the COVID isolation for a while, but the war finally destroyed the bonds between them.

The woman, who at first categorically forbade her husband to leave home, eventually began to humiliate and bully him for his cowardice. During their arguments, she would sometimes resort to forbidden tactics, labeling him as weak and unmanly. She would compare him to others, then apologize, exit their apartment, and vanish for the entire day, leaving him without an explanation, knowing he would not chase after her. This psychological cruelty became a routine feature of their monotonous provincial existence, a grim form of domestic entertainment. I was not quite tactful in asking for further details and gossip about Oleksandr and Solomiya because this seemingly banal story seemed to be a topic for a full-fledged novel. A novel about a war that penetrates everywhere, seeps into the strongest compounds, and destroys them from the inside. It destroys families, destinies, and lives, even when it does not bombard them with missiles. War is a virus without a vaccine or completely safe isolation in the homestead front.

In the novel that I had already begun to imagine and write in my mind, Oleksandr was destined to rise from the ashes after his divorce. Crushed like a rotten apple by the roadside, he had to hit rock bottom emotionally before finding the strength to get back up. The hero of my novel would enlist in the army on his own and undergo the hell of the front. Wounded and shell-shocked three times, he would return to Kyiv after the victory and be awarded one of the highest honors.

He would make one more attempt to rebuild his family with Solomiya, but their efforts would ultimately falter. After demonstrating his strength to her and regaining her respect, the man suddenly finds himself emotionally drained. He would decide to escape and continue living in isolation, haunted by harrowing dreams in which he relentlessly retrieves the lifeless bodies of his fallen comrades from the front lines.

It has the potential to become a compelling and realistic novel, successful in Ukraine and popular abroad, and it could even be made into a movie, with slight changes to give it a happy ending with a successful marriage and two children. Frankly speaking, though, I do not see the need to invent and "create" anything now. The role of a writer may well be reduced to simply "recording" real life during such terrible and crucial times, which is much more interesting and bizarre than any conceivable fantasy.

War raises a multitude of questions for everyone, but it also imposes requirements concerning the responsibility and maturity of creative individuals who communicate with a broader audience through their works. As a writer, for instance, I feel a sense of acute danger: when writing about war, you always run the risk of falling into one of two key traps. The first is the excessive glorification or romanticization of war, which can lead to overly simplistic, categorical judgments and overuse of pathos. Any author worth their salt is wary of this, as it is easy to become a propaganda tool, a mere cog in the information machine, and ultimately a predictable and uninteresting representative of the official creative establishment, like many writers were in Soviet times. But how (and should one) avoid this if you are a writer and what you do best is write? And why not do what you can do well during a terrible war, doing your part to help your country and save your people?

The second trap is boasting about one's truth-telling, trying to be more righteous than the righteous themselves when the writer derives satisfaction from his or her creative courage. They raise painful topics, ask uncomfortable questions, and have the power to criticize not the enemy but their own people as if they were swimming against the tide. It is an incredibly tempting stance to be distinct and esteemed, to set oneself apart from the crowd and pull no punches. At the same time, if you put your talent to use by criticizing your own people, wouldn't that be putting a nail in your own coffin? When starting a new page, you have the choice to write about a war hero who bravely stood up for us, or you can delve into the story of a deserter or traitor. Which of these narratives will contribute to boosting morale and align with our path to victory, as they often say in these times?

Creativity during wartime is a constant balancing act between self-censorship and responsibility—a navigation between personal intentions and the broader expectations placed upon you, akin to steering between Scylla and Charybdis. It's not surprising that in such circumstances, many writers opt to forego their writing pursuits and instead dedicate themselves to volunteer work or military service. They come to the conclusion that there are more important and useful things to do during the war than writing.

I cannot remember the source, but I came across the idea that if all writers and storytellers, in general, were to romanticize war less and describe only its horrible, bloody, stinking guts, humanity could finally break free from the cycle of wars that recur every few generations in almost every corner of the world. The logic is that by glorifying war heroes and victories, we consciously encourage future generations to repeat this vivid experience and have their own war.

While I acknowledge a partial truth in this statement, I ultimately disagree with it. I do not pretend to be a great thinker, but my personal reflections and observations lead me to believe that war is indeed a facet of humanity's social nature, much like evil is an inherent part of human nature. Human nature can be diverse; we are all unique and one of a kind, even when we exhibit striking similarities in certain aspects. Some individuals naturally possess more strength and courage, while others may appear more delicate and reserved yet exhibit exceptional intelligence. There are those who embody both bravery and intellect, while standing alongside them are individuals who may be physically less robust but possess unwavering determination. These combinations are abundant, and they can often be deceptive. At times, a quiet and introverted person can reveal their tenacity and determination when it matters most, even surprising themselves.

I have used this somewhat banal introduction to articulate an obvious thesis: people are different by nature, so everyone experiences war in their own way. Certain individuals are more inclined to fear and panic, while others seem to operate like drones in modern warfare. Determination and physical endurance are a significant advantage during war, but weakness or frailty is not an indulgence.

Let me give you an example. In the winter of 2022, Ukrainian social media was stirred up by a post in which a woman said that her boyfriend was "not born for war." In other words, his physical and psychological traits do not make him an ideal soldier, that is, he is much more useful as a civilian because he can create a marketable product and contribute a lot in tax, which the state needs to maintain an army that should consist of "ideal soldiers" who are obviously "born for war." Naturally, this deeply angered thousands of people whose own loved ones might also be more valuable in non-combat roles, and who have also experienced fear on the front lines. They never dreamed of having to kill their enemies, but it so happened that they ended up in the army and were now bearing the burden of it. Needless to say, these words were painful for those whose own sons, brothers, and husbands had died on the battlefront.

One of the most terrible consequences of war is the erasure of differences, peculiarities, and individuality. During wartime, you are not a writer, a farmer, or a businessman who pays a lot in tax. You are a target for a missile, a bullet, or shrapnel. A bomb does not care about your education or income, your mental state, gender, or readiness to fight. In Russia's all-out war against Ukraine, the targets are not only the army, but also the Ukrainian people, each and every individual, without exception. Hence the conclusion that everyone should be involved in the country's defense, not just Rambo-like men "born for war."

The war became a true litmus test for patriarchy as a concept, evolving into both the most significant crisis of masculinity and a celebration of it. After all, no matter what is said, men are primarily the ones who are fighting on the front line. Of course, there are a lot of women in the ranks of the Armed Forces of Ukraine and other units of the defense forces, many of whom are fighting in the most hellish parts of the front line; but men outnumber them.

In this sense, the war has strained gender relations in Ukrainian society. It once again revealed the long-known but often mocked thesis that both genders are equal but not identical. In the postindustrial Ukrainian society of the 2010s, it seemed that the roles of men and women were the same, as were professional opportunities, and all that remained was to achieve equality in wages, representation in government, and opportunities for self-realization.

The full-scale war catapulted us back to a more primal, if you will, state of being. Men inherently possess greater physical resilience and strength, making them the primary focus of compulsory mobilization under martial law, whereas women are traditionally entrusted with safeguarding children and tending to family and household responsibilities.

I understand that such pronouncements can upset many people, but the fact remains that war is pushing us backward, leading to regression and deterioration across all aspects of life. It is a return to times marked by a lack of security, shortages in electricity and fuel, and a descent into earlier, less advanced stages of societal development.

Viewed from this perspective, the war in Ukraine serves as a stark illustration for the West of what can happen to their societies if a major war breaks out, requiring more than just preexisting military reserves to achieve victory. It is a situation where individuals with no prior military experience, staunch pacifists, and members of creative communities find themselves compelled to abandon their former lives, take up arms, and get accustomed to dirt under their fingernails from digging trenches.

In the end, feminist organizations refrained from organizing demonstrations and protests against forced mobilization or the ban on men traveling abroad, as such discriminatory measures appeared tolerable under the exceptional circumstances of imminent peril. These extraordinary conditions and mortal threats have driven contemporary society back to a(n archaic) mindset where men assume the primary role of defenders.

The masculine image of this defender, nurtured in our collective imaginations by mass culture and Hollywood cinema, turned out to be quite different in reality. Ukraine is defended not by conventional-looking Bruce Willis types with bulging biceps and a perfect smile, but by ordinary working-class men with calloused hands or gray-haired men with beer bellies.

The paradox of this situation lies in the fact that the war has simultaneously become a celebration of masculinity and the source of its most significant crisis. It has confirmed the patriarchal foundations of society while also imposing a heavy burden on millions of Ukrainian women who went abroad alone with their children or were left without their husbands who were mobilized.

The war has unmistakably divided gender roles and profoundly altered the perception of various individuals within society. A man who volunteered for the army and has been at the front for a year and a half without a vacation has become a hero. Oleksandr, who had been hiding for a year and a half and did not leave his home, was treated as a virtual traitor, an object of social ostracism. It is not solely about gender; it is mainly about decency, civic consciousness, a sense of duty, and specific character traits, including courage. There are undoubtedly many heroic women who would not hesitate to go to the front if required, while others would desperately look for ways to avoid conscription. The difference, however, lies in the fact that the state put men to this test, not women.

Let me share a personal memory. In early March 2022, I brought my family to my hometown of Vynohradiv in southern Transcarpathia. Back then, the city had doubled in size, as so many internally displaced people had come there to escape the war and Russian occupation. One day, I took our daughter for a walk to the city center. I will never forget the feeling I had at the playground. Only women were around, and their eyes were full of mute reproach: *Why are you here?* Their husbands were either at the front or hiding from mobilization in their homes. At that moment, being a man was extremely embarrassing.

In the second year of the war, we are living in a situation where there are fewer men on the streets of Ukrainian cities than before. A significant number of them are serving in the military, but even more prefer not to go out into crowded places without reason, lest they accidentally run into a patrol of military enlistment officers. Perhaps many years after the war ends, Ukrainian history textbooks will write about how lines of volunteers formed in front of military commissariats, ready to defend their country and people, in the first hours of the Russian attack. I wonder if anyone will mention in even one sentence that a few months later, many more men were hiding and avoiding social life. Some were afraid of being drafted, while others were simply physically uncomfortable in the company of women whose sons, husbands, or brothers could be somewhere in the hell of the front.

Indeed, war is far more complicated than all the clichés suggest. It corrodes us from within, fosters feelings of hatred, and erodes human relationships with aggression. At a certain point, an enraged society can no longer refrain from seeking out those responsible and identifying an enemy. The air is saturated with malice and a desire for quick justice, and completely random people often become victims of this tension. A reckless word in an interview, a different tone of voice, a slightly more sophisticated thought, and a person is automatically subjected not just to criticism but attempts to "cancel" them.

The cases of Yuriy Andrukhovych, Yaroslav Hrytsak, and Oksana Zabuzhko, whom their own Ukrainian society tried to crucify as apostates or traitors, are very telling. Perform at a festival with the "wrong" person, give an interview to the "wrong" media outlet, publish a text in the "wrong" anthology—and the lynch mob shows no mercy. People who have been building modern Ukrainian culture and a modern European state for decades were suddenly declared enemies. And these tirades often contain more aggression in them than against the actual enemy. The pursuit of internal enemies is ongoing, and it is also remarkably convenient, as the potential victims are right here, in close proximity, just a comment away. We are familiar with them, making it effortless to inflict harm.

In the grip of daily stress and existential woe, society seeks avenues for psychological relief and ways to unwind. With an abundance of fear and anger in their lives, people instinctively seek outlets for these emotions, ultimately latching onto aggression. Subconsciously, they search for targets at which to release these pent-up emotions. Since the real enemy is distant, it is often relatives, friends, or even strangers, whose existence the justice-seeking individual just discovered on social media, that become the unwitting targets.

In such circumstances, everyone, without exception, gradually starts to be perceived as a coward, traitor, or enemy, not just individuals like Oleksandr who evade military service, but also ideological "saboteurs" like Andrukhovych or Hrytsak. Someone fought near Bakhmut, while someone else served in a less dangerous area. Someone volunteered, while someone else was forcibly mobilized. Someone was wounded, while someone else was just shell-shocked. Someone had their leg amputated, and someone was "unfairly" rewarded military honors. Ideally, there should be no room for disputes and accusations among those who wear military uniforms, but they persist, and they are alarmingly widespread. The contagion of aggression affects everyone and everything, eroding societal restraints across all strata of society. I am not writing this to excuse Oleksandr and his shameful and irresponsible yet somewhat comprehensible stance. I see him not so much as a coward or a traitor, but as a victim of war. He may not bear any visible wounds or injuries, but the war has already run him over with the tracks of a multi-ton tank and destroyed him. The law must provide a legal judgment of his actions, but from a human perspective, everything is more or less clear: he was a good, successful, and decent man. If it had not been for Putin and his army, Oleksandr would have lived a normal and fulfilling life and not become an object of ostracism and public contempt. Often, when we criticize or persecute some Ukrainians, we forget who is the main enemy and the cause of all our fears.

War is about more than heroes and valor. In essence, war touches every one of us, even those who are far from the front line and without shrapnel wounds. None of us were born for war; it is not in our nature. Yet, in different ways and to varying degrees, we all eventually become its victims.

Draft

For four years, eleven months, and two days, it rained in Gabriel Garcia Márquez's Macondo. And when it finally stopped, the people poured into the streets, rejoicing in the sun, paying no attention to the destruction and the hardships they had endured. How little it takes to feel joy—just a ray of sunlight. How little it takes to spark love . . .

"A war had to happen for me to fall in love with my hometown," says Kateryna, who was born in Popasna in Donbas three years after Ukraine declared its independence. A child of a free country, she, as long as she could remember, wanted to escape from her hometown. No, she didn't hate it, she just thought that life is given to us only once, and it shouldn't be lived in Popasna. Not in the middle of gray concrete and architecture in the style of the most primitive industrial brutalism. Not among the working class and all the shades of proletarian despair.

Accordingly, she built her life around this idea: she attended school and dreamed of enrolling in a university as far from home as possible. However, her parents insisted she not go too far, using persuasion and even emotional blackmail to make her apply to Donetsk University. This meant another five years of putting her life on hold and waiting for the moment she could leave with her degree for Kyiv or abroad.

"I didn't even come home for the biggest holidays," Kateryna continues. "Occasionally for Easter, once for my mother's milestone birthday, and I debated going to my best school friend's wedding, but later decided against it. What was there for me? Strangers, different interests, a town that felt practically foreign. It wasn't my fault I was born there. It's so painful to grow up watching one thing on TV while living in completely different circumstances. I didn't crave wealth so much as beauty: to live in a beautiful city, in a beautiful space, surrounded by beautiful people. That's why even Kyiv was just a stopover on my way abroad."

I met Kateryna when I picked her up in my car near the border. She was returning from Austria, and mutual friends had asked me to meet her and take her to the train heading to Kyiv. In the early days of the full-scale invasion, she had left the Ukrainian capital and ended up a refugee in Poland. Later, friends helped her find a job in Linz, Austria, so she relocated there. She lived among beauty—both natural and urban. As an architect, this was important to her.

But when life began returning to Kyiv in the early autumn of 2022, Kateryna decided to go home. Even if it meant enduring shelling and blackouts, she wanted to reconnect with her roots.

At this transit point in her life, we crossed paths, filling the hour-long drive from the Slovak-Ukrainian border to the Mukachevo train station with conversation. Kateryna was on her way home, though she didn't have a home in the sense of walls and a roof. Before the war, she had lived in Kyiv in a rented apartment because she wanted to be in the very heart of the city, but buying property there was still out of reach for her. For her, "home" meant Ukraine—specifically Kyiv. Her one true home had been in Popasna, in the Donetsk region, but it was destroyed by the Russians in May 2022.

I told her that I had been nearby—in Bakhmut—during those battles for Popasna. We had delivered volunteer aid to our soldiers and heard stories from each of them about Popasna and the villages around it. I'm not sure why I told her this. Maybe to ease my own conscience, to show that I wasn't indifferent, that I was there.

"Honestly, I'd love to live in Austria; it's a beautiful country," Kateryna said, as if justifying her return to Ukraine and soothing her own conscience. "If I had built a career and landed a job in Austria on my own, I would have been overjoyed. But as a refugee, forced to leave, I don't want to live abroad—it feels humiliating. It's as if I was driven out, got scared, and ran away. That's not how it's going to be. I even promised my mom that after the war, I'll earn enough money and build her a new house in Popasna. She was surprised: Why? Wouldn't it make more sense to build a house somewhere near Kyiv, where we could all live together, far from Russia? But I want to build in Popasna, even if I take my mom and we end up living in Kyiv. I miss Popasna, and I want us to have a little house there, a place to come back to on weekends or holidays. A place to call home."

A few minutes before the train's departure, I make her promise to give me a tour of Popasna after our victory. It's a ritual phrase, meant to encourage each other, like saying, "Next year in Jerusalem."

"I'm not sure if I'll be able to give you a tour," Kateryna admits hesitantly, "because I remember the city as if through a curtain of heavy rain." At that moment, I bite into a madeleine and feel transported to Macondo. "And everything there is destroyed now—just ruins. I've seen the photos; only the outlines of the streets remain. But I still miss those streets. I love my city deeply. It's so bittersweet to recall my childhood there, the lilacs blooming with their wild, intoxicating scent right outside my window."

Kateryna boards the train and heads to Kyiv. She's going home, though she no longer has a home.

The train ride lasts fourteen hours. But her journey will take much longer. After running away so many years ago, when will she finally feel like she has truly arrived home?

***

Impressed by the successes of the Ukrainian army—which came as a surprise to the enemy, allies, and Ukrainians themselves—global media and analysts point to the professionalism of Ukraine's armed forces, their disciplined training, and eight years of military reforms (counting from the first invasion of Ukraine in the spring of 2014). However, the real secret may lie elsewhere.

The Ukrainian military is so effective and capable because it is primarily made up of civilians. Yes, it's true that over eight years of hybrid war, Ukraine implemented significant defense reforms and built a military modern in both spirit and structure. Yet, it was still too small to resist a full-scale invasion.

Sevenfold—that's the number military analysts cite when discussing the expansion of Ukraine's military since February 24, 2022. This means that while the backbone of the armed forces is composed of well-trained professionals, the majority are made up of yesterday's civilians. These are people from all walks of life who lined up en masse outside recruitment centers in the early days of the invasion and the hundreds of thousands mobilized in the following months to reinforce military units.

Let's consider this again: the Ukrainian army is predominantly made up of civilians. Yes, these men and women now wear camouflage uniforms with insignias, receive salaries from the Ministry of Defense, and carry weapons. But they have civilian educations and backgrounds, and every one of them dreams of the war's end and returning to their normal civilian lives. Consequently, they view their military mission as temporary—a service with a clear beginning and end.

Teachers, foresters, IT specialists, doctors, drivers, bakers, managers, hairdressers, steelworkers, builders, stylists, waiters, singers, farmers—representatives of these and many other peaceful professions now form the backbone of the Ukrainian military. They fight temporarily, intending to return to their regular jobs. For them, war is a pause in their otherwise normal lives.

What does this mean in practice? People who weren't soldiers before 2022 try to bring their civilian skills and knowledge into their military routines. One might professionally construct a bunker, another can repair vehicles, a third bakes bread for the platoon, a fourth cuts hair, a fifth is great at social media and quickly raises donations for needed equipment, a sixth knows how to alleviate back pain from wearing body armor, and a seventh configures tablets for operating combat drones. Together, an entire unit is situationally better equipped to carry out assigned tasks and handle daily life because each soldier has a civilian profession in addition to their newly acquired military skills. In essence, these are people fighting with two skill sets.

This duality reveals two traits of the Ukrainian military—one positive and one negative. The downside is that these new fighters, not trained to traditional military standards, often struggle with the discipline required of their new role. However, the upside is their initiative, a quality that offers a decisive advantage as they frequently take responsibility at critical moments. This is a systemic strength over the Russian military, which mirrors its totalitarian society by suppressing initiative and relying on excessive centralization in all areas.

While a Russian soldier waits for orders from above, a Ukrainian fighter takes the initiative—making independent decisions, creatively leveraging available resources and weapons, improvising, adapting, and innovating to secure victory in battle.

The conversation also touches on motivation: Ukrainians have a clear understanding of why they are in the military —they are here to defend their land. This is an army of free people, instinctively reviving their archetype: the Zaporizhzhian Cossack Army.

It's an incredibly powerful archetype: an army of men who took up arms when necessary but, in times of peace, tended to their homesteads and worked the fields. They would sow and build when they could, but in times of danger, the saber was always within reach.

The image of the Ukrainian soldier today is that of a Cossack, fighting in the open steppe, yet dreaming of the comfort of home. The memory of home, the dream of home, nourishes him with strength. He also draws strength from the belief that the war is not forever—it is temporary. A time will come when he can return home.

***

Being in the army is like dying, my friend writes to me on the tenth month of his service in the Armed Forces of Ukraine.

I don't fully understand what he means, but I'm not sure how to ask delicately. It's late, he's far away, in the army, but I don't know if he's at the front right now. Maybe one of his brothers-in-arms has died? Maybe it's just exhaustion, burnout, depression?

If something happened to him, my asking could cause him pain. His message has already hurt me: because I'm at home, in relative safety, after a warm dinner, surrounded by loved ones. And he's somewhere unknown, in who knows what situation. More accurately, it's clear that his situation, in any case, is worse than mine. Because of that, I'm again overwhelmed by guilt and hesitate even more to reply. Eventually, I mark the chat as unread to give myself more time to think.

Finally, I ask directly: What happened?

He replies almost instantly: nothing special. It's just that when you've been away from your family for so long and can't visit, you sometimes feel like you've died and can only watch your family from the outside. How they live without you, solving problems you'd solve if you were home, missing you, and... continuing on with life. You can hardly influence it, but you can observe and communicate.

It's such a chilling image! Like something from a children's fairy tale, where the souls of the dead exist as angels beside us, observing, helping when needed, and guarding.

Modern technology allows us to experience separation caused by war in a new way. A few centuries ago, a soldier would receive no news from home, and his family would live in ignorance, waiting for the war to end. A century ago, soldiers wrote and received letters, keeping photos of their loved ones in their pockets.

But now, we can observe everything in real time. Chatting, sending photos, making video calls. Seeing that it snowed at home, and your wife has to shovel the driveway to take the kids to school in the morning. Watching your child change and grow day by day. Knowing what your family is having for dinner later that evening. Hearing that your neighbors painted their fence. Answering an urgent call when your wife is looking for the attic key.

Being in the army today means seeing your home, your former life, and your loved ones every day—but not being able to reach out. It's like watching a film in which you could have been the main character, but for some reason, you're not in the frame.

I wonder how often men experience the fear that, from a distance, someone else might take their place in the frame? This deeply personal and age-old fear of being replaced, of betrayal. And at the core of this fear is an existential question: Will life go on and be the same even if I die? The answer is clear: yes, it will. The answer is so painful that many people prefer not to ask themselves this question at all.

Modern warfare is the chance to operate drones and see enemy positions from many kilometers away. But at the same time, it's the chance to witness your life continuing somewhere without you. It's joy and sadness, closeness and alienation all at once.

Being in the army is like dying, my friend writes to me.

***

Mykola transports the dead; that's his job.

He is a serviceman, wears a uniform, and carries a weapon, but his role in the unit is to transport the deceased back home. He's not a medic, he doesn't retrieve the wounded from the trenches at the front lines, and he doesn't risk his life during combat. His mission is different.

On the one hand, it's a privileged and somewhat safer role, as most of the time he is on the road, far from the front lines. You're still in the military, but your chances of dying are lower than those of your fellow soldiers. On the other hand, I wouldn't wish such a privilege on anyone, not even the enemy: enduring dozens of hours on the road, knowing that behind you in the car is the body of a fallen brother-in-arms, someone you saw alive just days ago. And ahead of you lies the worst part—delivering the body and handing it over to the family. What words do you say at that moment? Where do you look?

From the front line to Uzhhorod, it's about fifteen hundred kilometers, a long way to go. Unfortunately, Mykola makes this trip often; he has a lot of work to do. Because of this, the vehicle requires regular maintenance and repairs: in a month, it covers the distance that other cars might drive in a year. It was during one of these repairs at a service station in Uzhhorod that Mykola and I met.

At first, I considered saving his name in my phone as Charon, but quickly changed my mind. In myths, Charon is grim and ominous, while my conversation partner seemed like a warm and friendly person. From the conversation, jokes, and occasional remarks from Mykola, I concluded that I was speaking with an educated and cultured individual. I'm almost certain he knows the reference and would likely be offended by such a nickname.

In fact, Mykola has a higher education and a fairly successful small business background. He has two children, one of whom already holds a higher education degree themself. He owns a house, a car, a passport with stamps from tourist countries, and all the other trappings of the middle class. But then the war came and put his entire life on hold. Mykola just laughs when I ask if he plans to stay in the military after the war ends.

A few months later, we meet again in Uzhhorod. I don't ask anything because I understand why Charon has crossed the river between the world of the living and the dead once again. But he begins to speak on his own, clearly needing to get something off his chest.

"Fewer people come to military funerals," he says. "At the beginning of the war, there were whole processions; people would kneel in the streets in front of the coffin, but now only relatives and colleagues show up. When I die, maybe no one will even notice, no one will come."

There is bitterness in his words. Not resentment or anger, but bitterness. Very personal, though it's somewhat tactless to think about one's own death while standing at someone else's funeral. But it's not narcissism or self-obsession—it's just that when a familiar person dies, a part of us dies with them. The death of others is always a prologue to our own death, a reminder that life only moves in one direction.

Mykola deals with the dead so often, it's as though he works for death itself. He hopes the war will end before it's his turn to cross the Styx.

***

When Roman put on his military uniform after February 24, 2022, he didn't know that within a year, he would die in that uniform. He liberated the south of Ukraine in it and went through the most harrowing ordeal of the war in Bakhmut at the end of December 2022. He could have died in close combat in Donbas, he could have stepped on a mine near Kherson, a Russian tank could have hit him, or an enemy drone could have dropped a grenade on him. In short, he had countless chances to perish in the war, but eventually, he simply died.

This semantic difference between "perished" and "died" confused those gathered to see their friend off in a small church on the outskirts of Uzhhorod.

On one hand, everything was clear—before us lies a hero, a man who voluntarily went to the military enlistment office in the early days of the war and headed to the front, even though he had been a civilian before.

On the other hand, Roman died of a heart attack at his unit's base, far from the front lines. While he formally (and factually) died in military uniform, it was not in battle.

This contradiction perplexed Roman's relatives and friends, who were preparing for the funeral. What protocol should be followed in this unusual situation? Fortunately, Uzhhorod was a day and a half away, so by the time Mykola brought the body, everyone had had time to discuss and reach a consensus.

Since the deceased did not die in battle, it wasn't appropriate to bury him in the local military cemetery's Alley of Heroes. But considering he passed away while serving in the military, far from home, it was decided to bury him in military uniform under the Ukrainian flag—just not at a military cemetery, but in a regular, civilian one.

Some were happy with this compromise, while others were outraged. The priest reconciled everyone, saying in his sermon over the casket that Roman had become a casualty of war. If it weren't for the war, the man would have stayed home, doing his regular civilian job drilling wells for artesian water. It was the war that became the burden that aged Roman in a year and exacerbated old health issues. What he had endured and witnessed in the year of war had killed him. The human heart wears out like a car part, but it can't be replaced under a warranty.

And yes, in war, people die "normal" deaths too, just like anywhere else. There is death in war—simple, banal, and unheroic. Not in battle, not from shrapnel, and not from a bullet, but from a sudden heart attack. "What bad luck," some said. "Now his family won't get compensation from the state. It would have been better if he had died in battle," others said.

A lot was said at that funeral. People stepped on the soft spring clay at the cemetery and irritably glanced at the priest, who seemed to be dragging the ceremony out.

When the first heavy lump of soil struck the coffin, sending a chill through everyone present, Mykola leaned toward me. "I don't know which sound is scarier: when a bomb goes off nearby or this," he said. And then he added, like an expert at a music competition, "After a year of hearing this sound, each time the soil hits the wood of the coffin, it's uniquely different in sound. Each strike is a unique sound. I don't know why I need to know this."

"Brothers and sisters," the priest said, looking around at everyone present. "Roman's earthly journey has ended. Roman has returned home."

***

When I'm asked which book one should read to understand the war in Ukraine, I always answer simply: the *Iliad*. There is no better or more complete encyclopedia of war for our civilization than this ancient epic. It contains all the plot twists, a range of motives, characters, and role models for the heroes of the centuries to come.

But what book should one read to understand life? The answer is similar: the *Odyssey*. For what is our life if not a grand journey through space and time?

The *Odyssey* can be interpreted in many ways: as an adventure story, as a moral parable about returning home, as a universal tale of a journey to oneself and the discovery of oneself within.

But one question remains unresolved: Does returning home signify harmony with the world around us and the discovery of our place within it? Or, ultimately, is it the end of the journey—the end of life itself—when clay and wood come together to create an irreplaceable, singular melody?

One could also say this about the *Odyssey*: It's fascinating to read, but who would want to go through all those trials and horrors themselves?

Now, as I write these lines, it is the 411th day of the war. Four hundred eleven days ago, we set out from our previous life toward some unknown destination, and we have not yet arrived there. We do not know when the war will end and peaceful life will begin again. Where are we heading? Toward the quick end of hostilities, or toward the start of an even bigger war, the Third World War?

We do not know—we currently exist somewhere on the road, in transit. Ukraine is often described as a country in-between—between East and West, between Europe and Asia. As if we are a bridge. It's a nice metaphor, but in practice, it's terrible because people don't live on bridges. It's impossible to live on a bridge. There, the winds whistle, it's uncomfortable and cold. There is a constant draft. A bridge is a structure for crossing, but not a home.

On February 24, 2022, all of us, Ukrainians, embarked on the scariest journey of our lives. We know when it started, but we don't know when or how exactly it will end.

A year, a month, and fourteen days of rain have poured over our Macondo. The downpour is so intense that we can no longer see our previous life. But we don't know when this rain will end. So we stand on the bridge, wet, hunched from the cold that pierces to the bones.

Frozen, grief-stricken, hardened along this journey of History, we peer ahead, seeking hopeful outlines in the rain's curtain. To end the odyssey and glimpse the home where we can finally arrive and find warmth.

For now, it remains out of sight.

A country of young widows

———

Some Ukrainian women donned camouflage, taking up weapons or tactical medical supplies. But the immense burden of war also fell on those who stayed behind. Men who were conscious, active, and relatively healthy went to the front en masse, leaving the home front largely in the hands of women. Of course, there are nuances, exceptions, and countless individual stories, but this is the broader reality.

Ukrainian women were already working, running households, and raising children before the war, but now many of them are forced to take on responsibilities that were typically carried out by men. From simple tasks like fixing a tap and mowing the lawn, to the need to earn more money while also spending more time with children who are deprived of communication with their fathers.

Very often, women—wives, mothers, daughters, and sisters of soldiers—take on another role: they volunteer, collect funds, and buy necessary supplies for the units where their loved ones serve. They also stimulate social changes, demand effective support for the army from local government authorities, organize community cleanups and public demonstrations, charity sales, and hospital shifts.

And, unfortunately, they find themselves young widows—women in the prime of their lives, holding young children and tasked with responsibility for their family's future, carrying on their husbands' legacy, and honoring their memory.

The story of Olena Zhuk, the widow of Junior Sergeant Roman Zhuk from the 128th Mountain Assault Brigade, is one example. Her husband was a photographer, videographer, and a member of the creative middle class. Together, they were agents of change in the provincial town of Mukachevo, eco-activists who inspired hundreds with their example.

The couple founded their own craft brand, Povna banka, under which they sold jam made from Carpathian berries. Olena and Roman also launched the chysto.de project, which was dedicated to cleaning Carpathian rivers and reservoirs of household waste and organizing eco-art picnics in the mountains for participants from all over the country. They were a successful and vibrant family.

In March 2022, Roman volunteered to go to the front. On May 26th of the same year, he was killed in combat in the southern Zaporizhzhia oblast. His wife, Olena, was left a widow, raising their two children on her own.

After her husband's death, Olena took on all the responsibilities of caring for the children, managing the household, and providing for the family. She continues to run their family business and actively develops the community initiatives they had started together, now in his memory. Additionally, Olena organized an event where she planted thirteen thousand tulip bulbs in front of the building of Mukachevo University, where she and her husband had studied and met. This alley is named after Roman Zhuk, and every year the tulips will bloom, delighting the eyes of all the townspeople.

It's quite possible that, in twenty years, a history textbook on Ukraine will illustrate the war with an image of a man firing from a self-propelled artillery gun. And that would be a great oversimplification, because while men defend the borders and the structure of the state, its true essence—the daily life that is Ukraine—rests on the shoulders of women.

The role of women in the daily life of not just families, but also communities and the state as a whole, has already grown incredibly during the war; and after victory, it will become—particularly in light of the demographic situation caused by frontline losses—a decisive one.

Astamur Humba ("Abkhaz")

It was one of the most difficult conversations in my life, even though it lasted only a minute and a half. I still replay it in my mind, unable to forget it, tormented by the thought of how I could have responded better. Ultimately, it was such a shock that I don't remember exactly how I responded.

There's nothing more terrifying than the words of a mother telling you that her son has died. Such words feel like a blow to the solar plexus, leaving you breathless and speechless. Because expressing sympathy in such a situation seems empty and futile.

In June 2022, the war was in full swing. I was contacted by Natalia Ishchenko, a well-known Kyiv-based analyst and journalist, with whom I shared a passion for the Balkans and had worked together with on the *Day* newspaper. Natalia told me that her son had volunteered for the army, and their unit was now stationed in the Kharkiv direction. One of their biggest needs was a vehicle for transporting personnel, as their unit was newly formed and lacked material and technical support. After I consulted with the soldiers, they decided that the best option for their work wasn't an SUV or a pickup truck, but a minibus, as it could fit nine soldiers and, if needed, transport personal belongings or even shells to the positions.

Natalia said she would raise the necessary funds for the minibus among her friends in Kyiv and asked me to find a vehicle and prepare it for deployment to the front. In about ten days, the vehicle was repaired and painted in camouflage

colors, and the minibus was ready to head east. Natalia and her husband, Serhiy, traveled to Transcarpathia to pick up the vehicle and drive it themselves, either to Kyiv or directly to Kharkiv oblast—it was an opportunity to see their son and his comrades. Along the way, they stopped to visit friends in the Carpathians and were planning to arrive in Uzhhorod the next morning.

That morning, I was abroad, having traveled to Slovakia to buy another vehicle for the army. The day before, I had informed the members of our team about the task and sent Natalia the address and contact information of the person she was supposed to meet to collect the minibus. Around 11:00 a.m., my phone vibrated: Natalia was calling, even though she had all the necessary information and knew I wasn't in Uzhhorod. I declined the call to avoid activating roaming charges. A few minutes later, she called again. When the phone rang for the third time, I realized it must be urgent and answered.

On the other end, I heard Natalia's bewildered voice. At first, I didn't understand what she was saying; her words were disjointed and chaotic. Then it hit me: she was apologizing for not being able to come and pick up the vehicle because it was no longer needed—her son, Astik, had been killed in the war. The grieving mother was in a state of shock, continuing to apologize while I struggled to find words. I muttered something about condolences and reassured her not to worry about the vehicle—we would deliver it to another unit. It was a horrific conversation, one I wish I could forget, but instead, I will have to live with it and replay it in my mind countless times.

This was our first loss on the front lines. I say "our" because our entire volunteer team felt it deeply. For three months, we had been working on getting vehicles for the army, and all our previous experiences had been joyful: here's the vehicle, we're heading east, meeting the soldiers, laughing, hugging, receiving their thanks, and feeling like we were doing something practical and genuinely helpful.

But then Ukrainian soldier Astamur Gumba was killed at the front. He already knew they would soon have a vehicle—his mother had even sent him pictures of it. But we didn't make it in time. And it felt like our loss. The searing thought haunted my conscience: if only we had acted faster, if only we had sped things up, maybe Astamur's unit could have escaped the shelling in that vehicle. Maybe he would have survived. Maybe...

Devastated by the situation, I became desperate to learn everything I could about Astamur Gumba—a defender of Ukraine who was both so ordinary and so extraordinary at the same time. His biography was the most striking part—worthy of a film or a book.

Astamur was born on July 22, 1989, in the city of Sukhumi. When he was three years old, war broke out in Abkhazia, forcing his mother to flee with him under the blasts of tank shells and grenades to Kyiv. Astamur grew up as a Ukrainian but took pride in his Abkhaz heritage, as the Gumba family has an ancient and well-known lineage in Abkhazia. Later, as a volunteer in the 130th Kyiv Territorial Defense Battalion, he earned the call sign "Abkhaz." He was killed on June 28, 2022, in Kharkiv oblast.

War seemed to cast its shadow over Astamur's life from the very beginning. When it returned, he faced it as an adult, choosing not to flee but to stand and fight. He didn't have to—he wasn't even a Ukrainian citizen. Yet, war caught up with him and claimed his life—a tragic chapter in the story of an ordinary yet extraordinary young man navigating the tumultuous post-Soviet landscape. It's a poignant drama of human existence at the crossroads of the violent twentieth and twenty-first centuries in Eastern Europe. One can't help but wonder how Astamur himself might have interpreted his fate. The thought is especially compelling given his university degree in philosophy—a discipline rarely pursued in today's world.

I'm not sure if it's appropriate to say this about a fallen hero, but Astamur doesn't look warlike at all in his photos. That's part of the profound tragedy: an intellectual young man with glasses, a wise, observant, slightly melancholic gaze—it's clear he was a sensitive soul. In one picture, he's in military uniform with a dog on his lap, smiling warmly, kind, and gentle. A kind-hearted philosopher who gritted his teeth and went to war, even though he should have been reading, traveling, falling in love...

It was our first loss. Sadly, there would be many more—now my phone is filled with the numbers of men I met near the front lines, men I embraced, whose hands I shook, with whom I laughed and posed for photos beside vehicles. Many of them are no longer alive, but that first loss burns the most. I never had the chance to meet Astamur, to get to know him. We simply ran out of time.

I feel a responsibility to tell this story, to share it so that the example of Astamur Gumba's sacrifice and courage is not lost or forgotten. There was a man in this world named Astik, call sign Abkhaz, a wise and kind-hearted young man—a philosopher. And if you are reading these words in Ukraine today, if you are alive, know that the hero Astamur Gumba gave his life for it. Remember him!

Youth

Our acquaintance got off to a rocky start. A little more and we might have ended up arguing. That's how it sometimes goes in text conversations—you miss the tone, the nuances of phrasing, or the subtleties of voice.

The story began when someone we both knew gave Vasyl, a scout with the 128th Mountain Assault Brigade, my number and told him I worked with vehicles. Vasyl messaged me, but his tone was off—as if he thought I was some kind of dealer he could buy a car from. When I explained that I *procure* vehicles rather than sell them, Vasyl shifted gears and started giving orders about what I should do for them. That threw me a bit, but in the end, we agreed to meet in person. Vasyl was due for a short leave and would be returning home to Mukachevo.

Two weeks later, we met over coffee at Café Snack in Uzhhorod. Vasyl came with his girlfriend. I was struck by how young he was—almost a boy. Lean, wiry, with a sharp, eagle-like nose—not at all how I had imagined the commander of a reconnaissance company in an elite assault brigade.

Talking with him wasn't easy. That's when I realized what had caused his bluntness in our earlier exchanges: Vasyl was a career soldier, and connecting with civilians didn't come naturally to him. He didn't know how to play the politeness game or fake a smile for appearances. He had just returned from the war—a place where everything is stark and unambiguous, where there's no gray area, only life and death. Even in the café, Vasyl couldn't sit still, shifting constantly in his chair. The civilian clothes and the peaceful atmosphere of Uzhhorod seemed to chafe against him.

After that conversation, I gathered the funds and bought a massive, badass-looking Dodge Jeep for Vasyl's unit. It was one of the best vehicles we had ever acquired for our team. We affectionately called it the "tank"—it was that powerful. In August 2022, along with a convoy of jeeps for other units, we headed south.

Our meeting took place in Zaporizhzhia oblast. The soldiers gathered, we handed over the vehicles, exchanged documents, took photos for reports, and chatted. Amid the bustle, Vasyl and his brothers-in-arms arrived. As he approached us, everything around seemed to quiet down in a cinematic way. Everyone turned to look at him; we were all drawn to his presence.

Now he was in his element: no longer the fragile, skinny guy, but a figure carved from stone and scorched by the southern sun. Fit, in uniform and tactical glasses, he walked toward us with a purposeful stride—like a movie hero, a god of war. Everyone around us fell silent, attentively listening to his every word. This is what it meant to be the commander of a reconnaissance company in an assault brigade. Fearless and proud, like every true scout. The elite of the army.

Vasyl Babych died three weeks later, in late August 2022, during a Ukrainian counteroffensive in Kherson oblast. He led his unit to clear the path for the infantry. Combat reconnaissance is one of the most perilous operations there is. He was only twenty-six and hadn't even started a family yet.

Getting to know Vasyl, I came to understand one of the key factors behind the success of the Ukrainian army. Born in Mukachevo, Vasyl Babych graduated from the Odesa Military Academy and was rapidly advancing in his military career. His youth and the remarkable responsibility of commanding a reconnaissance company symbolized a significant transformation within the Ukrainian army—its swift break from the remnants of the old Soviet system. Vasyl enrolled in the academy during the ATO in Donbas, fully aware that a frontline assignment, not a quiet post in the rear, awaited him. The new elite of the Ukrainian army was being forged, acutely conscious of the immense battle ahead to defend their country.

I had a similar experience in the early autumn of 2022. We had arranged a meeting with soldiers near the front line. When we arrived, a young guy in uniform approached me. I asked when the platoon commander would be there because we had some paperwork to sort out. "I'm the platoon commander," the young man said, stunning me.

It was Denys Samofal, a twenty-one-year-old fighter with the call sign "Talib." A native of Donetsk oblast, he graduated from the Lviv Military Academy of Ground Forces and, as a young officer, was thrown into the crucible of war. He died on October 15, 2022, during fighting in Kherson oblast. In July 2023, the president of Ukraine posthumously awarded Denys the title of Hero of Ukraine and the Order of the Golden Star.

Thirty years of independence gave us the opportunity to raise a new generation of Ukrainians who were born in a free country and cannot imagine any other fate. These individuals, born free, are now officers and soldiers fighting for their country as if it were something deeply personal—*their* Ukraine—not just a homeland from a folk song, but a private, cherished possession.

They fight and, tragically, die. Beautiful and young, like gods. Like the heroes in movies and books, who, to our fortune, are part of real life. Like Denys Samofal and Vasyl Babych.

Batia

At first, I was put off by his call sign.

"Batia" is derived from the word "dad" in Ukrainian, but in wartime, it also brings to mind a battalion. So, when a battalion commander has the call sign "Batia," it feels a bit odd. For one, it's overly predictable and clichéd. Additionally, military personnel typically come up with their own call signs, and if that was the case here, it seemed, at the very least, lacking in modesty.

But then, in the early summer of 2022, our communication became increasingly frequent, and I discovered just how amazing this person was. Batia, Colonel Mykola Krasivov, commanded the 105th Battalion of the 63rd Separate Mechanized Brigade. This unit was part of the reserve, formed and deployed after February 24, which meant it existed mostly "on paper." They recruited people, issued uniforms and rifles, but there was no strong organizational structure or logistical base. Everything had to be built from scratch, often relying on the military's own resources or turning to volunteers for support. That's how I met Batia.

By that time, the brigade had already been fully formed and had gone through its first baptism by fire in Volyn, near the Belarusian border. In the summer, the General Staff transferred it to the southern front to liberate the occupied parts of Mykolaiv and Kherson oblasts. The soldiers from this unit reached out to me for help with jeeps, and when I explained the need for document exchanges and acceptance acts, they gave me Batia's contact.

We communicated via Signal. I don't know how he managed it, but even from the very first messages—dry and official—Batia managed to create an atmosphere of friendliness and simplicity. You could tell he was a kind-hearted person with an easygoing nature. He knew how to emphasize how much he valued our volunteer work, and whenever something was required from him, he did it in a matter of minutes. I had communicated with so many commanders who I couldn't get a clear response or document from for months that, compared to them, Batia was a model of effective management.

That's why his battalion was fully equipped with everything you could imagine—from pickups and drones to the best canned goods, humanitarian aid, bulletproof vests, and even captured heavy weapons that he traded with other military units. A true leader, a skilled commander. What's more, there was a strong sense of order in his battalion, with a professional yet brotherly atmosphere. You could feel that everything about his unit was fair and honest.

For this reason, Batia was adored by his soldiers. Usually, in private conversations, soldiers don't hold back when it comes to criticizing their commanders, but here, there was admiration and almost a kind of filial love. No matter who I spoke with, everyone respected him and was proud of him. They knew that not everyone in the army was lucky enough to have such a commander. They respected him not only for his organizational talent but also for his courage: Batia didn't hide away and led his battalion into battle himself. He valued every soldier's life, knew how to stand up for his men, and never threw them into harm's way just to gain higher command's approval or a new rank.

For me and my team, he was our favorite commander, and his unit was the best. We loved to hold him up as an example for other military personnel, and we enjoyed visiting Batia. He always knew how to make us feel welcome, found time for a conversation, never forgot to say thank you, and, when needed, would show us the combat zone. He even found time to personally congratulate us on holidays. A sincere, cheerful person worthy of the highest praise. A natural leader, the soul of the team—in a word: Batia.

Colonel Mykola Krasivov died in November 2022 in liberated Kherson oblast, stepping on a mine, since he was, as always, the first to go to the front line, even before the sapper teams. A great man and a huge loss not only for his battalion but for the entire Ukrainian army.

Mykola Krasivov combined fierceness with simplicity, confident strength with human kindness. But God forbid you make him angry! Stocky, warm-hearted, and with a good sense of humor, he was also a bit feisty, just like a true Cossack. And his appearance had a distinctly Ukrainian vibe, like a guy you'd meet if you stopped in a village in Cherkasy or Vinnytsia to ask for directions; and there he would be, mowing the lawn in the yard.

Because of all this, you couldn't address him as "Colonel, Sir." It just felt natural to call him by the old Cossack term: "Batia." "Batia otamane," like in the folk song . . .

An icon painter

———

This Wednesday, I attended the funeral of a soldier. Let me tell you a bit about him.

Picture this: Chernivtsi, an international literary festival during the war, a sunny early September day in 2022. After my events, I finally get a chance to relax and sit down with a glass of white wine for an interview with a *Vogue Ukraine* journalist.

During the conversation, my phone starts vibrating. It was lying on the table, screen down, so it wouldn't distract us with notifications. As I continue talking about volunteering and literature, I flip my phone over and see a beautiful, naked woman on the screen. I quickly flip it back. In my shock, I didn't even manage to check who was calling.

After the interview, I move to a quiet corner and check my phone. A missed call on Telegram from Maksym Plesha. A soldier we brought a minibus to on the southern front in the summer. That's his profile picture—a naked woman, which is why that image popped up on my screen. I burst out laughing: well, I think, the military have their own jokes, good thing the journalist didn't notice, or she might have made assumptions about my so-called eventful life. I send Maksym an audio message, asking him to either text or call in the evening because I can't talk now. A few minutes later, I get a voice message in reply in broken Russian with a Caucasian accent—I'm told that this isn't Maksym, and if I want to know Maksym's fate, we can discuss it.

As it later turned out, that day the battalion Maksym served in took positions in a village near previously occupied Snihurivka in Mykolaiv oblast after an attack. Maksym moved to the frontline trenches with his ammo and the most essential items. Soon after, the Russians launched a counterattack and pushed our troops out of their positions. During the retreat, Maksym left his backpack with his belongings in the trench. It was in that backpack that the Chechens found the phone, from which they later called me.

The story was that the Chechens were trying to quickly call Maksym's contacts to tell them he was in captivity and demand a ransom. They needed to act fast, before Maksym could get in touch with his family from another phone. Since Maksym and I had been in contact the day before, the occupiers decided to call my number as well, not just his mother and relatives. And the nude picture on his avatar, which they found in one of the folders on his phone, was meant to show that they had complete control over Maksym's secrets, that he was in their hands.

Fortunately, Maksym didn't end up in captivity. We all laughed and breathed a sigh of relief. I saved the voice message from the Chechen because it felt like a touch from the other side—something slippery, cold, and unsettling, like hands reaching up from the grave. It was sickening to think that the dirty claws of the occupiers were rummaging through Maksym's personal belongings, looking through his messages with his loved ones, trying to access his online banking. But amid all the chaos, this story was soon forgotten.

At the end of autumn, after the liberation of Kherson oblast, in which Maksym took an active part, we met again. Maksym had come home on leave, and we met at a cozy café in Uzhhorod. I mentioned that at the end of the week, my team and I would be driving a convoy to the southern front, and it just so happened that Maksym was returning to his unit, so he came with us.

That trip also had its share of adventures: we accidentally left Maksym at a gas station in Mukachevo. Well, not exactly left—Maksym was supposed to switch to another car, but the driver of that car didn't know, so he drove ahead. Since there were ten cars and twenty drivers in our convoy, no one noticed the incident. Fortunately, Maksym quickly realized and called us to turn back for him. On that trip, we also celebrated my thirty-fifth birthday somewhere in a military hideout on the shores of the Dnipro Bay, opposite Crimea. I'm happy that Maksym shared that meal with us.

Later, Maksym's unit was moved to Bakhmut, where he went through hell, sustaining injuries and a concussion. He spent a long time recovering in the hospital, but even while bedridden, he tried not to waste time: he wrote to all the volunteers, asking for chemical warmers and thermal imagers for his brothers-in-arms, and did his best to help the soldiers with basic gear for winter combat. He had a big heart and a clear conscience—he felt ashamed to be resting while others were still fighting...

Our last chat was about his physical condition. After a year of hellish service in assault infantry, Maksym's health had deteriorated, and his injuries and traumas caused him serious complications. The biggest issue was with the ligaments in his legs and his ability to walk, but he didn't want to focus on it, insisting that he'd still be able to run one day!

I asked him if he was considering leaving the army due to his physical condition. Maksym replied that he might have wanted to, but he felt somehow ashamed in front of others. None of the people from his closest circle, those who went to war with him in the early days, had survived—they had all perished. He was tired, very tired, and wanted to rest a little, but he still didn't know what to do—he'd think about it later...

Maksym Plesha died in battle on August 23, 2023, in the Serebryanskyi Forest in Luhansk oblast. The enemy discovered their position and methodically shelled them with all types of weapons. After one of the explosions, Maksym's life was cut short. He had defended the Ukrainian border near Belarus, fought in the south, liberated Kherson oblast, and survived the hell of Bakhmut, but death found him on the Lyman front.

Maksym volunteered for the army, standing in line at the recruitment office, and on the third day of the war, he joined a mechanized unit, which was sent straight to the front lines. His reasoning behind his decision was simple: "How could I not go to war?"

In life and in spirit, he was an artist: gentle and a little shy. He painted icons, helped with church murals, and did portraiture; it was both a source of income and a personal passion. Before the war, he worked in a store to support himself and fund his painting, and in his free time, he'd sit in the city center, sketching portraits of people, often giving them the portraits as gifts. He was content with little, modest, and somewhat reserved. He was a simple, honest, and conscientious person—perhaps too much so for our sinful world.

At the funeral, I thought about how Maksym was completely out of place in the war. He and war were like two different worlds. Maksym shouldn't have died—he should have lived, painted, raised his daughter, created, built, explored.

He was buried in his hometown in a closed coffin. It was a shame because he was a handsome, well-built man. One could have painted portraits from someone like him . . .

Postscriptum

It's time to finish this book. What began as a story about the strength of people and their most beautiful impulses during this terrible time is slowly becoming a great Book of the Dead. Those I wrote about just a few months ago are perishing today; those you've just read about may be fighting their last battle tomorrow. Death plays with us, giving us brief moments of freedom before tightening its grip again, never allowing us to catch our breath. It continues to trap more and more new, beautiful, kind, and bright souls in its net... So, I ask you to close this book with one conviction: despite all the goodness and inspiration in the world, war remains humanity's greatest tragedy.

Acknowledgments

I would like to express my sincere gratitude to the Vienna-based Institut für die Wissenschaften vom Menschen and its Documenting Ukraine Program, PEN Ukraine, and House of Europe for their financial and organizational support during the work on this book. I am also sincerely grateful to my Patreon subscribers, because thanks to your support, I realized that this writing does make sense and is really needed by someone today. Thank you!

www.ingramcontent.com/pod-product-compliance
Lightning Source LLC
Chambersburg PA
CBHW020850160426
43192CB00007B/868